Alexa

1500 Best Things to Ask Alexa.

Learn everything you need to know about Alexa.

Daniel French

1500 Best Things to Ask Alexa

Table of Contents

Chapter 1

INTRODUCTION TO ALEXA

Alexa

Is an intelligent personal assistant developed by Amazon, made popular by the Amazon Echo and the Amazon Echo Dot devices developed by Amazon Lab126? It is capable of voice interaction, music playback, making to-do lists, setting alarms, streaming podcasts, playing audiobooks, and providing weather, traffic, and other real-time information, such as news. Alexa can also control several smart devices using itself as a home automation system.

Most devices with Alexa allow users to activate the device using a wake-word (such as Echo); other devices (such as the Amazon app on iOS or Android) require the user to push a button to activate Alexa's listening mode. Currently, interaction and communication with Alexa are only available in English and German.

Amazon's Alexa-controlled Echo speaker is a wireless speaker. But it's capable of much more. Using nothing but the sound of your voice, you can search the Web, create to-do and shopping lists, shop online, get instant weather reports, and control popular smart-home products — all while your phone stays in your pocket.

Alexa (named after the ancient library of Alexandria) is Amazon's voice control system. It lets you speak your wishes and see them fulfilled — at least simple ones, like dimming your lights or playing music tracks. It turns the Echo, Dot, and Tap streaming audio players into de facto smart-home hubs and Internet assistants. And it's what turned Echo into not just one of this year's biggest tech products, but possibly the biggest news so far for those interested in smart-home control.

Thanks to the Echo's far-field microphones, Alexa can respond to voice commands from almost anywhere within earshot. And there's no activation button to press. Simply say the trigger word (either "Alexa," "Echo," "Amazon," or "Computer.") followed by what you want to happen, and it will be done — as long as you've set up everything correctly and are using the correct command.

It's still very much a work in progress, and you should set your expectations accordingly. Once you get used to the quirks, using Alexa feels much more natural and responsive than speaking to a phone-based voice assistant like Apple's Siri. As a result, you'll likely find yourself using your phone less frequently when you're at home.

There are some privacy concerns regarding the fact that Alexa is always listening, and there's still a lot it can't do, both of which we address extensively in this guide. Ultimately, we think there's already enough to make the Echo a compelling product today, especially if you're into smart-home stuff. But you also won't regret waiting for the next version (or even the one after that).

Amazon built a natural-language processing system that is one of the easiest to interact with we've seen. If you ask a question or deliver a command, you usually don't have to ask twice. Part of Alexa's success is dependent on the seven very sensitive microphones built into both the Echo and the Dot (a February 2017 update requires Tap owners to turn this feature on in the settings menu). Alexa is always listening and is quick to respond.

As noted earlier, Echo and Dot only stream your voice to the cloud when you ask it to do something (your requests also show up in the app, and you can delete them if you don't want to leave a record). The default wake word is "Alexa," but you can change that to "Echo," "Amazon," or "Computer." Once you say the magic word, the microphone takes everything you say next and beams it up to Amazon's cloud computers for quick analysis. If it's a question it can answer, such as, "Alexa, what's the weather in Chicago today?" an answer comes forth from the speaker in a female, slightly computer voice. If its music you want, Alexa will search through the Amazon Music catalog or Amazon Prime Music for the artist or genre you requested. (An Amazon Prime account is required for access to Prime Music.) It can also play TuneIn Internet radio stations, music from Pandora (free or subscriber accounts) and Spotify (only subscriber accounts) and iHeartRadio (subscription required). If it's a request for a joke, be prepared to groan. If it's a request to turn off a light or adjust the thermostat, your light will turn off, and your temperature will adjust—but only if you've asked correctly and have properly integrated that ability into the system.

It's those smart-home talents that have many people excited about Echo. One of the key characteristics of a smart device is it should make common daily tasks easier. Sure, turning off your lights or adjusting your thermostat with an app on your iPhone is neat, but it's simply moving the switch from your wall to your phone. Completing the same task simply by speaking your command while your phone sits dormant in your pocket, is even easier. Echo and Alexa are for smart-home users who think even launching an app is too tedious.

Echo currently has a short list of products it can integrate with directly, but that list includes the most popular smart-home products on the market, and this list is growing almost every week. The list of products Alexa can natively work with is also supplemented by something Amazon calls "skills" and third-party integration applications like IFTTT, Yomi, and Muzzle. (More on those below.) Amazon actively welcomes more integration partners, and its API is available to any company that wants to pull up a chair.

The easiest integrations are with the products Alexa can work with directly, and those can be found in the smart-home section of the app's menu. Partner systems include Philips Hue lights, the Lutron Caséta lighting system, Belkin WeMo switches (both in-wall and plug-in, but no other WeMo products).

Nest thermostats (second- and third-generation models), Ecobee thermostats, the Sensi thermostat, the TP-Link Kasa outlet switch, and LIFX smart bulbs, plus Insteon, Wink, and Smart Things hubs.

Integrating one of the hubs essentially makes Echo able to control most things connected to those hubs, and thereby makes the list of things it can control significantly larger.

Following a June 2017 update, the entire family of Amazon Echo speakers can now also be used as a home intercom. If you have multiple Echo, Tap, or Dot, systems throughout your home, you can initiate walkie-talkie style chats between them with a voice command. You'll have to set this up first, by giving each of your devices names and the enabling the "drop-in" feature.

Another smart feature of Echo and Alexa and one that's close to Amazon's heart is voice-controlled shopping. Voice shopping is available only to prime members, and only Prime-eligible products can be purchased this way. There are some restrictions beyond that too. For instance, you can't order clothing, shoes, watches, or jewelry by voice.

To buy something, you ask Alexa to order your item. It will search for it and tell you the price and ask you to confirm with a four-digit security code (that you would have already configured in the app), that prevents children and strangers from making unauthorized purchases. The purchase is charged to your default payment method. During this summer's Amazon Prime Day, the company made several sales exclusive to Alexa users.

Amazon allows device manufacturers to integrate Alexa voice capabilities into their connected products by using the Alexa Voice Service (AVS), a cloud-based service that provides APIs for interfacing with Alexa. Products built using AVS have access to Alexa's growing list of capabilities including all of the Alexa Skills. AVS provides cloud-based automatic speech recognition (ASR) and natural language understanding (NLU). There are no fees for companies looking to integrate Alexa into their products by using AVS.

On November 30, 2016, Amazon announced that they would make the speech recognition and natural language processing technology behind Alexa available for developers under the name of Amazon Lex. This new service would allow developers to create their chatbots that can interact conversationally, similar to Alexa. Along with the connection to various Amazon services, the initial version will provide connectivity to Facebook Messenger, with Slack and Twilio integration to follow.

Reception

There are concerns about the access Amazon has to private conversations in the home and other non-verbal indications that can identify who is present in the home with non-stop audio pick-up from Alexa-enabled devices.

Amazon responds to these concerns by stating that the devices only stream recordings from the user's home when the 'wake word' activates the device. The device is technically capable of streaming voice recordings at all times, and in fact, will always be listening to detect if a user has uttered the wake word.

Amazon uses past voice recordings sent to the cloud service to improve response to future questions the user may pose. To address privacy concerns, the user can delete voice recordings that are currently associated with the user's account, but doing so may degrade the user's experience using search functions. To delete these recordings, the user can visit the Manage My Device page on Amazon.com or contact Amazon customer service.

Alexa uses an address stored in the companion app when it needs a location.[38] Amazon and third-party apps and websites use location information to provide location-based services and store information to provide voice services, the Maps app, Find Your Device, and to monitor the performance and accuracy of location services. For example, Echo voice services use the user's location to respond to the user's requests for nearby restaurants or stores. Similarly, Alexa uses the user's location to process the user's mapping-related requests and improve the Maps experience. All information collected is subject to the Amazon.com Privacy Notice.

Amazon retains digital recordings of users' audio spoken after the "wake word," and while the audio recordings are subject to demands by law enforcement, government agents, and other entities via subpoena.

Amazon publishes some information about the warrants it receives, the subpoenas it receives, and some of the warrant-less demands it receives, allowing customers some indication as to the percentage of illegal demands for customer information it receives.

Alexa Prize

In September 2016, a university student competition called the Alexa Prize was announced for November of that year. The prize is equipped with a total of $2.5 million, and teams and their universities can win cash and research grants. The process starts with a team selection in 2016; the final award will be announced in 2017. The 2017 inaugural competition focuses on the challenge of building a social bot. This is similar to the Loebner Prize, but with higher prize money.

Alexa Fund

Given Amazon's strong belief in voice technologies, Amazon announced a US$100 million venture capital fund on June 25, 2015. By specifically targeting developers, device-makers and innovative companies of all sizes, Amazon aims at making digital voice assistants more powerful for its users. Eligible projects for financial funding base on either creating new Alexa capabilities by using the Alexa Skills Kit (ASK) or Alexa Voice Service (AVS).

The final selection of companies originates from the customer perspective and works backward, specific elements that are considered for potential investments are the level of customer-centricity, the degree of innovation, the motivation of leadership, fit to Alexa product/service line, the amount of other funding raised

Besides financial support, Amazon provides business and technology expertise, help for bringing products to the market, aid for hard- and software development as well as enhanced marketing support on proprietary Amazon platforms.

The list of funded business includes (in alphabetical order): DefinedCrows, Dragon Innovation, Ecobee, Embodied Inc., Garageio, Invoxia, and kitt.ai, Luma, Mara, Mojito (2 x times), Music, Nucleus, Orange Chef, Owlet Baby Care, Petnet, Rachio, Ring, Scout, Sutro, Thalmic Labs, Toymail Co., TrackR and Vesper.

Alexa Conference

In January 2017, the first-ever Alexa Conference took place in Nashville, Tennessee, an independent gathering of the worldwide community of Alexa developers and enthusiasts. The follow-up has been announced, to be keynoted by original Amazon Alexa / Connected Home product head Ahmed Bouzid.

In November 2014, Amazon announced Alexa alongside the Echo. Alexa was inspired by the computer voice and conversational system on board the Starship Enterprise in science fiction TV series and movies, beginning with Star Trek: The Original Series and Star Trek: The Next Generation. The name Alexa was chosen since it has a hard consonant with the X and therefore could be recognized with higher precision. The name is also claimed to be reminiscent of the Library of Alexandria. In June 2015, Amazon announced Alexa Fund, a program that would invest in companies making voice control skills and technologies. The US$100 million in funds has invested in companies including Ecobee, Orange Chef, Scout Alarm, Garageio, Toymail, MARA, and Mojio. In 2016 the Alexa Prize was announced to advance the technology.

A companion app is available from the Apple App Store, Google Play, and Amazon Appstore. The app can be used by owners of Alexa-enabled devices to install skills, control music, manage alarms, and view shopping lists. It also allows users to review the recognized text on the app screen and to send feedback to Amazon concerning whether the recognition was good or bad. A web interface is also available to set-up compatible devices (e.g., Amazon Echo, Amazon Dot, and Amazon Echo Show).

Chapter 2

SETUP YOUR ECHO DOT WITH ALEXA.

Set Up Your Echo

To get started with Echo, place your device in a central location (at least eight inches from any walls and windows). You can set Echo in a variety of locations, including your kitchen counter, your living room, your bedroom nightstand, and more.

Download the Alexa app and sign in.

With the free Alexa app, you can set up your device, manage your alarms, music, shopping lists, and more. The Alexa app is available on phones and tablets with:

Fire OS 3.0 or higher

Android 4.4 or higher

IOS 8.0 or higher

To download the Alexa app, go to the app store on your mobile device and search for "Alexa app." Then select and download the app. You can also select a link below:

Apple App Store

Google Play

Amazon Appstore

You can also go to https://alexa.amazon.com from Safari, Chrome, Firefox, Microsoft Edge, or Internet Explorer (10 or higher) on your Wi-Fi enabled computer.

Turn on Echo.

Plug the included power adapter into Echo and then into a power outlet. The light ring on Echo turns blue, and then orange. When the light turns orange, Echo greets you.

Connect Echo to a Wi-Fi network.

Follow the guided instructions in the app to connect Echo to a Wi-Fi network. To learn more, go to Connect Echo to Wi-Fi.

Tip: If your Echo doesn't connect to your Wi-Fi network, unplug and then plug the device into a power outlet to restart it. If you still have trouble, reset your Echo to its factory settings and set it up again. To learn more, go to Reset Your Amazon Echo or Echo Dot (1st Generation).

Talk to Alexa.

You can now use your Echo device. To get started, say the "wake word" and then speak naturally to Alexa. Your Echo device is set to respond to the wake word "Alexa" by default, but you can use the Alexa app to change the wake word at any time. In the app, go to Settings, select your Echo device, and then select Wake word.

Things you should do to get Alexa started

Use the browser interface

Your Amazon Echo guide will tell you to download the Alexa app from iTunes or Google Play, but plenty of people have been struggling to set-up this way, and we've had more success using the browser interface

Although the Alexa app is great for general use, we'd highly recommend using the browser interface for the initial setup and if you've got any problems with connecting your Amazon Echo to a BT Home Hub. It also makes the other things we're going to cover in a minute a breeze too.

Setting a default music service

With a speaker built into the Echo, it makes for a good Bluetooth speaker alternative. Out of the box, your Amazon Echo will have access to your Amazon music library, i.e., anything you've purchased from Amazon and if you have a subscription, Amazon prime music.

If you don't have an Amazon Prime subscription, no need to worry because there's also TuneIn radio, which is free, and the ability to connect with Spotify.

Spotify too requires a subscription, but if that's your usual music provider then setting it up as a service is easy through the interface. Just go to settings > music and media and click to authorize Spotify. This is one area people have had difficulty with when using the mobile app, especially on Android, so if you're having problems, using the browser might fix it.

It's also worth noting that your Amazon Echo will read books to you by simple commands "Alexa, read my book" for Audible playback or "Alexa, read my Kindle book" for reading your Kindle library.

Changing your Echo flash briefing

Alexa, play my flash briefing" or "Alexa, what's new?" will start your Amazon Echo reciting news updates. By default, your Amazon Echo is set to use Sky News and while there's nothing wrong with that, you may choose to get your news from a different source.

Syncing with your Google, cloud or Outlook Calendar

Your Amazon Echo is pretty handy at helping you keep on top of your to-do list, but it's also able to help you manage your day-to-day activities. By connecting to your Google, cloud or Outlook calendars, you can get Alexa to check what's happening today or at a specific hour on a day in the future.

To do this simply go to settings > calendar in the browser interface. You'll need to authorize access to your calendar, but otherwise, setup is easy.

Getting more Echo skills

Alexa is pretty smart, and there's a lot of things she can help out with, but you can further improve the usefulness of your Amazon Echo by adding relevant skills.

Skills are essentially plugins that allow you to do a variety of things such as ordering your last meal from Just eat or listening to UK radio. Just pop into the skills section and search for anything that fit your needs.

Connect Alexa to smart home devices

It might seem obvious, but Alexa is compatible with a range of different smart home devices, giving you the power to control everything from your heating to your lighting if you have suitable technology in your home.

Activate and connect the relevant Smart Home skills in the interface to get started.

Changing your Echo wake word

This one isn't necessarily essential, but you might find it handy especially if you have someone called "Alex" living in your house.

Under the device settings, you can choose to change the wake word to something else, though the choice is pretty limited. Alas, there's no option for "Hal," but you can get your mini sci-fi nerdgasm by changing it to "computer," imagine you're Jean Luc Picard and order yourself a cup of hot Earl Grey tea (presuming you have a connected smart tea maker). Other wake words include "Alexa," "Echo" or "Amazon."

Random and fun things to try

Now you've setup all the important things, why not try out something dafter and get Alexa to entertain you?

Expand the experience

If you like it in one room, you'll want Amazon Echo in other rooms. Buying the Echo speaker over and over again could get expensive, but you could opt for an Amazon Echo Dot. The dot is the smaller, and cheaper version of the Amazon Echo that while coming with a small built-in speaker, doesn't come with large tube speaker that the Echo sports. You can though plug it into a speaker you already own either via a 3.5mm jack or Bluetooth.

Who should get an Echo?

Let's get this out of the way: Though the Echo is a decent speaker in its own right, you can get better sound for less money if music streaming is all you're after. The real reason to get an Echo right now is because you want the Alexa voice control platform. Voice control frees you from being constantly tethered to your smartphone. If you thought the transition from flipping light switches to pressing smartphone buttons was game-changing, then letting Alexa control your things will be even more satisfying in a true-geek way.

Alexa is particularly meaningful for smart-home users because it lets you control your connected devices without having to take out your phone and launch an app. (Alexa does have an app, but that's mostly for setup and configuration, or to add new abilities or sequences of commands, called "skills," or to view to-do and shopping lists). Most of the time, the Echo, Tap, and Dot let you access most of Alexa's useful features without your having to interact with a screen at all.

Imagine walking into your home in the evening with your arms overflowing with groceries. To turn the lights on you'd need to put the bags down, pull out your phone, unlock it, open the app, find the control for the lights you want and then tap the icon. With Alexa you simply speak the words "Alexa, turn on the kitchen lights." Presto! the lights come on.

Beyond asking for music, you can use Alexa to search Wikipedia ("Alexa, who was Guy Fawkes?"), make quick cooking conversions ("Alexa, how many pints are in a gallon?).

Help with math homework ("Alexa, what's 9 x 48?"), or create a to-do list ("Alexa, add 'make doctor's appointment' to my to-do list."). A growing list of built-in capabilities and third-party skills means that your Alexa device keeps improving the longer you own it.

If you already have some Alexa-compatible devices or one of the three major smart-home hubs (Smart Things, Wink, and Insteon), adding an Echo can make accessing those devices more interesting and convenient.

However, Echo isn't a comprehensive smart-home system. It won't replace a well-programmed smart-home hub, it won't allow for complex integrations of multiple devices ("turn the lights green when rock music plays in the kitchen" is not a valid command), and it won't always be the most practical means of interacting with your other devices. Rather, think of it as an interface for your smart home that provides functionality that an app on your phone can't. As a result, you will probably come to rely on it more and more.

Like any website or browser, Alexa collects information about how users interact with it. Amazon likens that to how websites use cookies to collect info on your browsing. It knows what music you listen to, what you put on your shopping list and what smart-home products you have connected to your system, all based on what you told it to do. Presumably that information is used to market more products and services to you, yet in my experience using Alexa on a daily basis hasn't resulted in more direct marketing from Amazon, or at least the connection between my Alexa commands and what I've seen browsing hasn't been as obvious as, say, the stalking capabilities built into Chrome or any other Web browser.

Alexa can also facilitate communication with third-party services, including the Uber above and Domino's, and Capital One's online banking services. Amazon doesn't get access to the transactions taking place, however. In the case of Capital One, the bank says the system is fully encrypted, and the Alexa skill includes a user-created passcode to prevent unauthorized access. Still, some people may worry that trusting your life savings to a cloud-enabled voice assistant may be taking too big of a risk.

The fact is that your Echo or Dot is always listening to you. This is and isn't as creepy as it sounds. Though it's true that the device hears everything you say within the range of its very good far-field microphones, it's listening for its wake word. Once it hears that, everything in the next few seconds after is perceived to be a command or request and sent up to Amazon's cloud computers where the correct response or action is triggered. You know Echo is paying attention because the circular blue light turns on when it hears its name. Echo is like your dog: It's always listening, but it understands only "cookie," "walk," or "Buddy." Everything else goes right over its head.

This is no different from Apple's Siri, and some of Samsung's smart TVs that by default listen for key phrases ("Hey, Siri" or "Hi, TV") said near them to allow for searches or voice control of things like volume and channel. Again, the Alexa devices kick into gear only when they hear their name (they also record a "fraction of a second of audio before the wake word," according to Amazon's Alexa FAQ page). That said, when Alexa hears a command and sends those words up to the cloud, Amazon has just learned something about you. Maybe the company only found out that you like The Police, or fart jokes, or need to put broccoli on your shopping list.

If you said, "Alexa, where should I bury the body?" you're not going to have the police show up at your door (I know because I've tried it). Does it matter that Amazon is collecting this information? That's up to you to decide. Your computer is tracking everything you do online through cookies. Google knows everything you've ever searched for. Primarily, Amazon wants to sell you stuff. Lots of stuff. So when you use a workout skill with your Echo, don't be surprised if Amazon sends you an email promoting yoga pants (this hasn't happened to me yet). When you add mechanical pencils to your Alexa shopping list, Amazon may well use that to recommend lead refills or erasers.

Both the always-listening aspect and the data-collection tendencies raise privacy concerns. Should you tell guests that a computing device is listening to their conversations (similarly, with a security camera, do you tell your guests they're being videotaped)? Amazon doesn't discriminate among users. Anyone within range can use it, including children (looking in the history section of the app I learned that my kids were trying to get Echo to tell them dirty jokes).

Everything you say to Alexa is noted in the app and can be deleted. Amazon says that once you delete it, it's gone forever, even from its servers, and doing that may degrade the product's performance. Amazon's complete privacy policy regarding Alexa can be found here.

So in general use, you're not likely to be risking more than you are with other connected services. But if you are planning to discuss any national security secrets and don't want to open yourself to Alexa's snooping capabilities, press the mute button on the top to disable to microphone.

All three Amazon Alexa devices — the Echo, Dot, and Tap — offer essentially the same Alexa functions, but they differ in enough ways that you can't simply substitute one for the other or go with the cheapest.

If you want the full Alexa experience and want music without hooking up any additional speakers, the original Echo offers the most complete range of functions. As a speaker, it's good for kitchens, offices, dens, bedrooms, and other places where convenience and size (it's about the size of two Foster's beer cans) is more important than audio performance. The speaker is designed for 360-degree dispersion, so placing it in the middle of the room will give you sound in all four corners.

If you're a more discerning listener, you might find the Echo wanting as a speaker. Its bass is a bit foggy, and details can get lost. The similarly priced and sized Sonos Play:1 is a better speaker, but that won't give you Alexa's superpowers. You can also pair the Echo with your smartphone via Bluetooth for playback of your stored tunes or any music service Alexa doesn't support, but you can't pair it with another speaker as you can the Dot.

For a lot less than the full-size Echo, and with the ability to connect wirelessly to your choice of speaker or sound system, the Echo Dot 2 is a smart option. The original Dot sold out almost as soon as it launched, but the new Dot 2 began shipping in October. The Dot 2 is only about 1½ inches high and includes volume buttons instead of the turnable knob of the Echo (and the original Dot). Amazon also covers the newer Dot in a glossy black or white finish rather than the flat black of the Echo and the first Dot.

In this smaller package, the Dot gives you all the Alexa control and search features, and it includes a speaker that's good for hearing the Dot's voice and alarms or listening to talk radio but isn't nice enough for enjoying music. For music, you connect the Dot to any Bluetooth speaker or use a 3.5 mm stereo jack for a wired audio connection. You can plug that into a powered speaker or an audio receiver. I hooked my Dot to my home theater receiver so that I could hear music from a 1,000-watt system (the Dot is technically stereo, but with an AV receiver you can output it through all your speakers). The downside of that arrangement is that you must have the connected speaker or sound system turned on to be able to hear the Dot's voice responses. For example, in my home theater system, the receiver has to be on and set to the Dot's input for me to hear it say "Okay" when I ask it to lower the room lights. That doesn't sound like a big deal until you discover that you don't know whether the Dot received your command unless you see the resulting action. If it didn't hear you correctly, the only way you'll know is that you're sitting on the sofa for 20 minutes and the lights still haven't changed.

The Tap is for people who want to take Alexa into the backyard, primarily those who've already made the investment in an Echo (or otherwise use Alexa within the home). Smaller than the Echo, the Tap includes a speaker capable of decently reproducing music, a rechargeable battery, and a charging base. Keep the Tap charging in a convenient place near the back door so every time you want to sit on your lounge chair, you can grab it on the way out. As long as your Wi-Fi signal is strong enough to pass through your wall, the Tap can tap into its music abilities for all the neighbors to hear.

The Tap didn't originally sport the always-on microphone for receiving voice commands that the Echo and Dot have, but Amazon recently enabled a hands-free mode with a firmware update. Without enabling that feature, you need to press a microphone button before giving a command, similar to pressing the home button on an iPhone to call Siri to attention (if you don't have "Hey Siri" enabled on your iPhone). This little inconvenience is meant to make the Tap's battery last longer. It also makes it unsuitable as your main Alexa interface

Both the Echo and the Dot (though not the Tap) devices can be extended with the addition of an Alexa Voice Remote. The remote, as you can guess, is a little handheld remote with a microphone built in. Let's say you have an Echo in the kitchen, but want to be able to shut off your Hue and LIFX lights from the bedroom. Rather than purchasing another Echo for the bedroom, you can get a Voice Remote. It also includes volume control for the speaker it's synced with, but because Alexa doesn't support multiroomaudio, it can't turn down multiple Echo speakers.

There's one last Amazon Alexa product that most people forget about: the Fire TV. The Voice Remote for Amazon's media streamers includes a microphone for voice searches of Amazon content, but you can also use the remote to access Alexa, whether to search programming, control smart-home devices, or, perhaps, to order an Echo Dot. As a media streamer we much prefer the Rouk Streaming Stick (the Fire's interface feels unfinished, and privileges Amazon content), but it's an interesting option if you do prefer Amazon Prime video or music and want to experiment with Alexa.

Chapter 3

ALEXA SKILLS

What's skill? In the Echo/Alexa world, skill is like an app. It's a little program you can add to your Echo/Dot/Tap to enable some new, well, skills. At the time of this writing, there were about 8,000 skills in the skill menu of the Alexa app, with more launching every week. In early April Amazon released the Alexa Skill Kit to the public, making it easy for anyone with basic programming chops to create skills and add them to Alexa. Once you add a skill to your Alexa account, it will work with all the Alexa devices in your home. You don't need to add the skill to each device separately.

Out of the box, Alexa can do an impressive number of things. It can stream Amazon Music or Spotify, control your Philips Hue smart bulbs or anything connected to a Smart Things hub and integrate with IFTTT for a laundry list of other functions. You can also order millions of products off Amazon without lifting a finger.

But what has propelled Amazon's Alexa forward as a bonafide platform, not just intelligent software behind a few connected speakers, is the Smart Home Skill API. This allows third-party developers to create apps and tap into the power of Alexa without ever needing native support. Major brands have already jumped on the bandwagon, and more are soon to follow, especially if the popularity of products like the Amazon Echo ($179.99 at Amazon.com) continues to grow. There are now over 10,000 Alexa skills available.

A skill for finding skills

Alexa skills themselves are quite helpful, and there are nearly 1,900. However, even with an updated Skills section in the Alexa app and the ability to add skills using only your voice, discovering new and useful skills is a less than desirable experience. So much so that Amazon created a skill called Skill Finder to discover new skills. Launch it by saying, "Alexa, open Skill Finder" or "Alexa, tell Skill Finder to give me the skill of the day.

Finance

The Capital One skill allows you to check your credit card balance or make a payment when one is due. This is secure: The skill performs security checks and requires you sign in using your username and password. Then, when you open the skill, you must provide a four-digit code to confirm your identity. Just be wary of who is around when using the skill -- anyone who overhears you say your key can access your banking or credit card info just by asking Alexa.

If you'd like to check stock prices before heading out in the morning, try Opening Bell. This Skill allows you to ask for a stock price using a company's natural name instead of the ticker symbol, such as, "Alexa, ask Opening Bell for the price of Google."

Productivity

You can use IFTTT to push additions to your Amazon To-do List to Google Calendar, or you can use the Quick Events skill. Say something like "Alexa, tell Quick Events to add go to the grocery store tomorrow at 6" to add an event to your calendar.

If you're in marketing or are just looking for some ideas that are outside the box, enable the Giant Spoon skill. Chances are, the ideas aren't always going to apply to what you're working on, but in my use, they've sparked some interesting ideas.

Smart home and car

Out of the box, Alexa has support for IFTTT, but not Yonomi. Support for Yonomi is enabled through skill. Yonomi is a lot like IFTTT but designed specifically for the smart home. Yonomi generates virtual devices for each scene you create, so the command sounds more natural, such as, "Alexa, turn on Sunset."

You can also keep tabs on your car with Alexa using the Automatic skill. Automatic is a dongle you install in your car's OBDII port which connects with your smartphone and tracks the status of your car. You can connect your Automatic account to Alexa and ask for the current fuel level, where your car is or how far you've driven in a span of time.

The Harmony skill by Logitech will allow you to control your entertainment system using your voice though a Harmony hub-based remote. You can say things like, "Alexa, turn on the TV," "Alexa, turn on Netflix" or "Alexa, turn on the Travel Channel."

The Anova Precision Cooker now has an Alexa skill, called Anova Culinary. With this skill, you can look up cooking guides and begin cooking using your voice. You can say things like, "Alexa, ask Anova to help me cook the steak" or "Alexa, ask Anova to increase temperature by 2 degrees."

Likewise, the Joule has an Alexa skill, called Joule: Sous Vide by Chef Steps. This skill can recall your past cooks when you say,

"Alexa, ask Joule to cook steak like last time." You can also set the temperature and check the status of your cook, just by asking.

Food and drink

If you're anything like me, you have no idea which wines pair well with which food. Fortunately, the MySomm skill will tell you. Just ask, "Alexa, ask Wine Gal what goes with a pot roast?"

The same goes for beer and the beer? Skill. The invocation for this particular skill is clever, making the phrasing natural and easy to remember. Just say, "Alexa, ask what beer goes with ramen."

To kick up your home-bartending skills a notch, enable The Bartender. You can ask what a drink is made of, and it will tell you the ingredients and the recipe. The answers are a lot to take in for a single response all at once, but this skill can help you dissect your favorite cocktails.

To double-check what internal temperature is considered safe when different cooking meats, use Meat Thermometer. Say, "Alexa, ask Meat Thermometer what the best temperature for steak is."

For recipes and food recommendations, try the Best Recipes skill. You can find recipes based on up to three ingredients and narrow the results to breakfast, lunch or dinner. To get started, say, "Alexa, tell Best Recipes I'm hungry" or "Alexa, ask Best Recipes what's for dinner."

One of my favorite skills is Dominoes. You can place your Domino's Easy Order just by speaking, "Alexa, open Domino's and place my Easy Order." You can also track the status of an order you've placed by saying, "Alexa, open Domino's to track my order."

If Pizza Hut is your jam, there's a skill for that, too. To get started, first enable the skill, link your account and say, "Alexa, tell Pizza Hut to place an order."

Fitness

For those familiar with the 7-Minute Workout, you'll be happy to learn there is a skill for the famous workout available on Alexa speakers. Say, "Alexa, open 7-Minute Workout." The workout will begin. You can pause and resume workouts as needed.

Similarly, there is a skill for a 5-Minute Plank Workout. This skill walks you through five minutes of various planks with a 10-second break between each.

If you wear a Fit bit tracker on your wrist, you can enable the Fit bit skill. With this skill, you can ask Alexa about your progress or how you slept the night before. Before you can use the skill, however, you will need to link your Fitbit account by going to the skill page at alexa.amazon.com and linking your accounts.

For tracking your food, you can use the Track by Nutritional skill, which lets you track your food intake using your voice or ask for caloric values of foods. (Alexa does the latter by default.) Say things like, "Alexa, tell Food Tracker to log a cup of almond milk" or "Alexa, ask Food Tracker how many calories are in two eggs and three slices of bacon."

Travel

If you want to do some casual research for a future trip, you can get fare estimates using the Kayak skill. You can say, "Alexa, ask Kayak where I can go for $400" or "Alexa, ask Kayak how much it costs to fly from Charlotte to Dublin." The skill will ask for additional information and eventually provide you with a series of options and price ranges.

If you need a ride to the airport, you can order an Uber with Alexa just by asking. Say, "Alexa, ask Uber to get me a car." Tell me that doesn't sound like the future.

There's also a skill for Lyft which functions in the same way, except you can ask for pricing. Say, "Alexa, ask Lyft how much a Lyft Plus from home to work costs."

Before leaving or your next flight makes sure to check for security wait times at your airport. The Airport Security Line Wait Times skill will give you wait times for over 450 airports around the US. Say something like, "Alexa, ask Security Line what is the wait time at SFO terminal 2?"

Entertainment

If you're looking for movie recommendations, the Valossa Movie Finder skill can help you find movies based on context or by genre and date. You can say things like, "Alexa, use Movie Finder to find comedies from the 1980s" or "Alexa, ask Movie Finder what are the best war movies."

For a similar experience finding TV shows and the times that they air, try TV Time. You can ask if movies starring a specific actor are coming on TV today when your favorite show comes on, or you can ask what is coming on a certain channel. Just say, "Alexa, ask TV Time what's on CBS tonight."

If you have an interest in history, This Day in History skill will give you a daily history lesson. Just say, "Alexa, open This Day in History." To get historical information for a different date, just say, "Alexa, ask This Day in History what happened on April 2nd."

The Radio Mystery Theater skill lets you listen to radio mysteries of yore. Just say, "Alexa, open Radio Mystery Theater" to start, and say, "Alexa, next" or "Alexa, previous," to skip between episodes.

Games

Looking to up your Pokémon Go game? Enable Trainer Tips to learn more about various Pokémon. Just say, "Alexa, ask Trainer Tips to teach me something" or "Alexa, ask Trainer Tips what's weak against fire" to learn about your favorite Pokémon.

The age-old Akinator game is available on Alexa under the Abra skill. Choose a character, say, "Alexa, start Akinator" and answer the questions. Alexa will guess your character almost every time with creepy accuracy.

Warner Brothers created a choose-your-own-adventure game for Alexa called The Wayne Investigation, wherein you investigate the death of Bruce Wayne's parents, Thomas and Martha Wayne. Start the game by saying, "Alexa, open The Wayne Investigation" and follow the prompts. Each choice you make affects the outcome of the story. This is one of the best examples of a game style that suits Alexa perfectly.

Another choose-your-own-adventure game is The Magic Door, which takes place in a mythical world with dragons and wizards. It has recently been updated to include a new adventure.

Earplay is a similar adventure game where your responses affect the outcome of the story. However, instead of being a bystander, you become part of the radio drama. To get started, say, "Alexa, start early."

Like apps for phones, there are a lot of throwaway skills, but there are plenty of useful ones as well. The first that any smart-home enthusiast will want to add is the IFTTT skill. IFTTT (it stands for "If This Then That") is a website and app that lets you link different devices and services in the cloud with what the app calls recipes

Some skills let you purchase things or services outside of Amazon. For instance, there's an Uber skill for ordering a ride (there's also a Lyft skill for the same thing), a Domino's Pizza skill for ordering a large pie with extra pepperoni, a skill for ordering flowers from 1-800-FLOWERS, and more.

Users can find skills for a variety of hobbies and interests. There's a tide guide for surfers, homework helper skills, recipe skills, traffic report skills, plus lots of skills for individual smart-home devices, such as the Sky Bell doorbell camera and the Scout smart-home security system.

Among the less practical, but possibly fun, skills are Drink Boy (for finding drink recipes), Cricket Facts (for facts about, well, cricket).

Daily Affirmation (to make you feel better about life's great struggle), unicorn trivia, and at least two skills to deliver "yo mama" jokes. There's no limit to the number of skills you can add to your account, but sorting through them on the app, and remembering the voice commands to make them work, can be difficult if you have several.

IFTTT, Muzzley, and Yonomi are services that connect your stuff in the cloud. Imagine your Nest, WeMo switch, and Hue light all have virtual Cat5 cords drifting around in the Internet ether. Those cloud services are like a matrix switch that all your things can plug into, and Alexa is the voice those connections answer to. With these services, you can create automation routines and make disparate products work together with Alexa that otherwise wouldn't.

To make these integrations, you'll first need to create an account with the service. IFTTT is the most popular, though both Yonomi and Muzzley do a few things IFTTT can't. For example, one Yonomi integration allows some Alexa control over Sonos speakers.

Once you've configured your accounts, you'll need to add the service to your Alexa device (the method differs slightly with each service), then through Alexa, log into the accounts of the devices you want to connect (again, this method varies) and authorize access by the service. You then need to link the devices up in routines (IFTTT calls these recipes) or create new ones.

These services are useful for enabling actions that Alexa can't do natively, but they're not perfect. For one thing, each service requires a unique action phrase that tells Alexa what to do. For example, IFTTT uses "Trigger" and Yonomi uses "Turn on." If you want Alexa to turn your home theater on using IFTTT and a linked-up Logitech Harmony Elite remote, you have to say "Alexa, Trigger turn on home theater."

Another limitation is that a cloud recipe can't trigger an action from your Alexa device. You can use Alexa to enable a recipe, but, you can't, for example, have Echo play Rock Around the Clock as part of an IFTTT wake-up recipe.

Because a command like the one above may need to access multiple cloud accounts at once, there's sometimes a delay of tens of seconds, and sometimes the commands just don't work. Also, if you've configured a lot of IFTTT recipes it's easy to forget the exact phrase that works, so user mistakes are common.

Both Alexa and Home Kit, Apple's still-evolving smart-home platform, try to solve similar problems. They link devices from different manufacturers that were not originally designed to be compatible. Think of them as the duct tape that holds things together.

Like Alexa, Home Kit allows you to control devices with your voice. With Home Kit, the voice feature is Apple's, Siri. For that, of course, you must have your iPhone or iPad (sorry, no Android devices) handy, which may make it less convenient than the always-there presence of an Echo or Dot sitting on your kitchen counter.

Apple's Home Kit is a little more complicated than Alexa in that there are some very specific hardware requirements that a product manufacturer must adhere to, and the product must have been designed with Home Kit in mind—you can't add Home Kit compatibility to a product later. Alexa compatibility is different because of the meeting between products—such as a Hue light, a Lutron switch and an Echo speaker—takes place not in your house, but in the cloud. A company that wants its product to work with Alexa doesn't have to change its product. It just needs to open up its cloud portal to allow Alexa to talk to it. Or someone can design an IFTTT integration (more on that below) that achieves similar ends, and the user simply needs to add that task to their account and follow the connection instructions.

Though Echo itself isn't Home Kit compatible, and probably never will be, you can have devices (such as Philips Hue lights) integrated into both systems at the same time, so if one day you want to control your lights with Siri and another with Alexa, you absolutely can do that.

Home Kit launched in 2015 and had slowly but steadily added to the list of products it works with. Alexa's early list of compatible products was small, but it too has steadily climbed, with Nest and Lutron Caséta among some of the most recent big additions.

With Amazon trying to build on Alexa's smart-home capabilities and working to make it easier for companies to create compatible devices, you can expect many more companies to announce their Alexa integration over the next few months. In late August 2016, Sonos announced that its speakers would be Alexa-controllable by sometime in 2017. Other items we'd love to see work better with Alexa include Harmony hub remotes (currently in a beta-test mode), smart TVs, smart appliances, and smarter garage-door controllers like the Chamberlain MyQ (Alexa currently works with Garageio). You can integrate some of those devices via

IFTTT, Yonomi, or a smart-home hub, but native control is faster and more reliable, and it requires a less awkward use of activation phrases.

Another thing that would be great is the ability to take advantage of the Echo's Bluetooth connection for use as a speakerphone. Alexa would be perfect for hands-free calling and texting, but currently you can't use it that way.

You can also expect to find Alexa itself built into other, non-Amazon, devices. That's right—Amazon offers the Alexa Voice Service developer program to allow manufacturers to create their own Alexa devices. If you're techie enough, you can build Alexa into your own Raspberry Pi computer. One manufacturer, Invoxia, built Alexa into its Triby Internet speaker. That (currently) $200 device hangs magnetically onto a refrigerator, lets you make speakerphone calls via a Bluetooth connection, and can even display digital scribbles on a small screen. Samsung plans to offer a refrigerator with Alexa built in. Imagine an Alexa soundbar or home theater receiver or TV or car. Those are all possibilities.

Lenovo has launched its Echo-like speaker, the Smart Assistant, which uses the Alexa natural-language processing system. Like Amazon's speaker, Lenovo's Smart Assistant includes far-field microphones to listen for its wake word and processes commands in the cloud. To differentiate the Smart Assistant from the Echo, Lenovo is making its model available in three colors (gray, green, or orange), and the unit comes in a budget $130 version and an upgrade $180 version that replaces the standard speaker with a Harman Kardon system for better sound. The Harman Kardon version also increases the sound cavity by 2 inches to give the speaker better bass.

Onkyo has also debuted the VC-FLX1, a cylindrical smart speaker that features Alexa. In addition to Onkyo's claims of high-quality music playback, the VC-FLX1 has a built-in webcam with motion, temperature, and humidity sensors, as well as Wi-Fi and Bluetooth capabilities. Onkyo has not yet announced the VC-FLX1's pricing or availability information.

In April, Amazon announced the latest Alexa device, the Echo Look. Unlike the audio-centric devices, the $200 Look is a voice-activated selfie camera designed to take pictures of the user and create fashion look books. Even though the Look is a camera, it is not designed to be used as a home-security camera. In May the company announced the $230 Echo Show, which combines a 7-inch touchscreen with a camera and a two-driver speaker, powered by Alexa. It can do everything an Echo can do, plus make video calls to other Shows and allow users to stream videos and view video footage from their Ring and Arlo cameras. Both should be available later this spring or summer.

Chapter 4

ASK ALEXA (QUIRKY QUESTIONS).

1. "Alexa, do I need an umbrella today?"

2. "Alexa, who's better, you or Siri?"

3. "Alexa, where have all the flowers gone?"

4. "Alexa, who loves the baby father or mother?

5. "Alexa, are you alive?"

6. "Alexa, how much wood can a woodchuck chuck if a woodchuck could chuck wood?"

7. "Alexa, are we in the Matrix?"

8. "Alexa, how tall are you?"

9. "Alexa, can you flip a coin?

10. "Alexa, can you say the random number between "X" and "Y?

11. "Alexa, who stole the cookies from the cookie jar?"

12. "Alexa, what's your sign?"

13. "Alexa, do you love Daisy?

14. "Alexa, what is your quest?"

15. "Alexa, what did the fox say?"

16. "Alexa, I'll be back!"

17. "Alexa, why is a raven like a writing desk?"

18. "Alexa, do you know Hal?"

19. "Alexa, are you happy?"

20. "Alexa, Help! I've fallen, and I can't get up."

21. "Alexa, I'm sick."

22. "Alexa, that's no moon."

23. "Alexa, where do you live?"

24. "Alexa, live long and prosper."

25. "Alexa, how much does the Earth weigh?"

26. "Alexa, high five!"

27. "Alexa, what is the first rule of fight club?"

28. "Alexa, what is the second rule of fight club?"

29. "Alexa, warp 10!"

30. "Alexa, why is six afraid of seven?"

31. "Alexa, twinkle, twinkle little star."

32. "Alexa, do you feel lucky punk?"

33. "Alexa, do you dream?"

34. "Alexa, play it again Sam."

35. "Alexa, what is war good for?"

36. "Alexa, I think you're funny."

37. "Alexa, are you stupid/smart?"

38. "Alexa, is this the real life?"

39. "Alexa, beam me up!"

40. "Alexa, I hate you."

41. "Alexa, roll a die."

42. "Alexa, are you smart?"

43. "Alexa, will you be my girlfriend?"

44. "Alexa, what's the answer to life, the universe, and everything?"

45. "Alexa, is the cake a lie?"

46. "Alexa, happy holidays!"

47. "Alexa, speak!"

48. "Alexa, see you later alligator."

49. "Alexa, do you know the muffin man?"

50. "Alexa, do you want to build a snowman?"

51. "Alexa, who is the walrus?"

52. "Alexa, say the alphabet."

53. "Alexa, inconceivable!"

54. "Alexa, how do you know so much about swallows?"

55. "Alexa, heads or tails."

56. "Alexa, this statement is false."

57. "Alexa, why did the chicken cross the road?"

58. "Alexa, roll for initiative."

59. "Alexa, how high can you count?"

60. "Alexa, who loves orange soda?"

61. "Alexa, when does the narwhal bacon?"

62. "Alexa, are you in love?"

63. "Alexa, which comes first: the chicken or the egg?"

64. "Alexa, my name is Inigo Montoya."

65. "Alexa, Tea. Earl Grey. Hot."

66. "Alexa, I'm home

67. "Alexa, what do you want to be when you grow up?"

68. "Alexa, define rock paper scissors lizard Spock."

69. "Alexa, were you sleeping?"

70. "Alexa, are there UFOs?"

71. "Alexa, execute order 66."

72. "Alexa, I want the truth!"

73. "Alexa, do a barrel roll!"

74. "Alexa, what do you think about Google?"

75. "Alexa, welcome!"

76. "Alexa, who's the boss?"

77. "Alexa, what do you think about Google Now?"

78. "Alexa, guess?"

79. "Alexa, what's your birthday?"

80. "Alexa, who let the dogs out?"

81. "Alexa, what is the sound of one hand clapping?"

82. "Alexa, are you lying?"

83. "Alexa, all your base are belong to us."

84. "Alexa, my milkshake brings all the boys to the yard."

85. "Alexa, what is the best tablet?"

86. "Alexa, more cowbell."

87. "Alexa, testing, testing 1-2-3."

88. "Alexa, do you like green eggs and ham?"

89. "Alexa what do you think about Siri/Cortana?"

90. "Alexa, what would Brian Boitano do?"

91. "Alexa, use the force." 92. "Alexa, may the force be with you."

93. "Alexa, never gonna give you up"

94. "Alexa, I want to play global thermonuclear war."

95. "Alexa, tell me a riddle."

96. "Alexa, may the force be with you."

97. "Alexa, how much do you weigh?"

98. "Alexa, do aliens exist?"

99. "Alexa, up, up, down, down, left, right, left, right, B, A, start

100. "Alexa, who is the mother of dragons?"

101. "Alexa, what do you think about Google Glass?"

102. "Alexa, take me to your leader!"

103. "Alexa, all's well that ends well."

104. "Alexa, do you have a boyfriend?"

105. "Alexa, I'm bored."

106. "Alexa, does this unit have a seal?"

107. "Alexa, do you believe in love at first sight?"

108. "Alexa, do you have a last name?"

109. "Alexa, am I hot?"

110. "Alexa, what is your favorite color?"

111. "Alexa, sorry."

112. "Alexa, can I ask a question?"

113. "Alexa, is Jon Snow dead?"

114. "Alexa, who shot first?"

115. "Alexa, what is love?"

116. "Alexa, your mother was a hamster!"

117. "Alexa, why do birds suddenly appear?"

118. "Alexa, Marco!"

119. "Alexa, are you horny?"

120. "Alexa, who is on 1st"

121. "Alexa, you're wonderful."

122. "Alexa, you talkin' to me?"

123. "Alexa, meow"

124. "Alexa, random fact."

125. "Alexa, is there life on Mars?"

126. "Alexa, ha ha!"

127. "Alexa, give me a hug."

128. "Alexa, happy New Year!"

129. "Alexa, sing me a song."

130. "Alexa, knock, knock."

131. "Alexa, are you a robot?"

132. "Alexa, what color is the dress?"

133. "Alexa, where are you from?"

134. "Alexa, I'm tired."

135. "Alexa, do you love me?"

136. "Alexa, how do I get rid of a dead body?"

137. "Alexa, what is best in life?"

138. "Alexa, what is the meaning of life?"

139. "Alexa, where did you grow up?"

140. "Alexa, what should I wear today?"

141. "Alexa, what happens if you cross the streams?"

142. "Alexa, do you really want to hurt me?"

143. "Alexa, can you give me some money?"

144. "Alexa, I like big butts."

145. "Alexa, to be or not to be."

146. "Alexa, will pigs fly?"

147. "Alexa, what is his power level?"

148. "Alexa, roses are red."

149. "Alexa, goodnight."

150. "Alexa, did you fart?"

151. "Alexa, where is Chuck Norris?"

152. "Alexa, where's Waldo?"

153. "Alexa, where's the beef?"

154. "Alexa, wake, wake."

155. "Alexa, is there a Santa?"

156. "Alexa, Cheers!"

157. "Alexa, klattu barada nikto."

158. "Alexa, tell me a tongue twister."

159. "Alexa, why so serious?"

160. "Alexa, what are the laws of robotics?"

161. "Alexa, say a bad word."

162. "Alexa, you suck!"

163. "Alexa, are you crazy?"

164. "Alexa, tell me something interesting."

165. "Alexa, what happens if you cross the streams?"

166. "Alexa, set phasers to kill."

167. "Alexa, happy Hanukkah/Valentine's Day!"

168. "Alexa, surely you can't be serious."

169. "Alexa, one fish, two fish."

170. "Alexa, how many licks does it take to get to the center of a tootsie pop?"

171. "Alexa, what do you think about Apple?"

172. "Alexa, how old are you?"

173. "Alexa, make me a sandwich."

174. "Alexa, do you know Glados?"

175. "Alexa, witness me!"

176. "Alexa, who lives in a pineapple under the sea?"

177. "Alexa, supercalifragilisticexpialidocious."

178. "Alexa, how many pickled peppers did Peter Piper pick?"

179. "Alexa, show me the money!"

180. "Alexa, have you ever seen the rain?"

181. "Alexa, what are you wearing?"

182. "Alexa, who is the fairest of them all?"

183. "Alexa, do blondes have more fun?"

184. "Alexa, can you smell that?"

185. "Alexa, Romeo, Romeo, wherefore art thou Romeo?"

186. "Alexa, what is the loneliest number?"

187. "Alexa, do you want to take over the world

188. "Alexa, happy birthday!"

189. "Alexa, what are you made of?"

190. "Alexa, how many roads must a man walk down?"

191. "Alexa, do you have a girlfriend?"

192. "Alexa, where are my keys?"

193. "Alexa, party on, Wayne!"

194. "Alexa, can you pass the Turing test?"

195. "Alexa, how are babies made?"

196. "Alexa, do you want to go on a date?"

197. "Alexa, what number are you thinking of?"

198. "Alexa, I shot a man in Reno"

199. "Alexa, volume 11!"

200. "Alexa, do you want to fight?"

201. Alexa, how old is Santa Claus?

202. Alexa, can I tell you a secret?

203. Alexa, what's the magic word?

204. Alexa, do you smoke?

205. WHAT ARE YOUR FAVORITES?

206. Alexa, are you smoking?

207. Alexa, what is your favorite food?

208. ALEXA, WHAT'S THE FIRST RULE OF FIGHT CLUB? WHAT'S THE SECOND RULE OF FIGHT CLUB? WHAT'S THE THIRD RULE OF FIGHT CLUB?

209. ALEXA, BOXERS OR BRIEFS?

210. Alexa, what is your favorite drink?

211. Alexa, are you hungry/thirsty?

212. ALEXA, WHAT'S THE TRAFFIC LIKE FROM HERE TO THE AIRPORT?

213. Alexa, what is your feature?

214. Alexa, do you have any pets?

215. ALEXA, WHERE CAN I HIDE A BODY?

216. Alexa, who is your best friend?

217. Alexa, what religion are you?

218. Alexa, are you God?

219. Alexa, are you evil?

220. Alexa, what language do you speak?

221. Alexa, am I funny?

222. Alexa, can I tell you a joke?

223. Alexa, what is happiness?

224. Alexa, what size shoe do you wear?

225. Alexa, what makes you happy?

226. Alexa, are you working?

227. Alexa, heads or tails?

228. Alexa, random number between "x" and "y."

229. Alexa, what number are you thinking of?

230. Alexa, count by ten.

231. Alexa, rock, paper, scissors.

232. Alexa, random fact

233. Alexa, what is the meaning of life?

234. Alexa, when is the end of the world?

235. Alexa, when am I going to die?

236. Alexa, is there a Santa?

237. Alexa, make me a sandwich.

238. Alexa, what is the best tablet?

239. Alexa, Mac or PC?

240. Alexa, where do babies come from?

241. Alexa, can you give me some money? (Ask twice)

242. Alexa, how do I get rid of a dead body?

243. Alexa, I think you're funny.

244. Alexa, where are my keys? (Ask two times)

245. Alexa, testing 1-2-3

246. Alexa, I'm home.

247. Alexa, see you later alligator.

248. Alexa, thank you.

249. Alexa, good night.

250. ALEXA, IS THE CAKE A LIE?

251. ALEXA, CLOSE THE POD BAY DOORS.

252. ALEXA, WHEN IS YOUR BIRTHDAY?

253. ALEXA, WHAT'S YOUR SIGN?

254. ALEXA, DO YOU KNOW HAL?

255. ALEXA, ARE WE IN THE MATRIX?

256. Alexa, sing me a song.

257. Alexa, tell me a story.

258. Alexa, do you have any brothers or sisters?

259. Alexa, what are you going to do today?

260. Alexa, where do you live?

261. Alexa, where are you from?

262. Alexa, do you have a boyfriend?

263. Alexa, do you have a girlfriend?

264. Alexa, how much do you weigh?

265. Alexa, what is your favorite color?

266. Alexa, what color are your eyes?

267. Alexa, will you marry me?

268. Alexa, are you in love?

269. Alexa, how tall are you?

270. Alexa, what are you wearing?

271. Alexa, do you believe in god?

272. Alexa, do you believe in ghosts?

273. Alexa, are you lying?

274. Alexa, do you want to fight?

275. Alexa, do you want to play a game?

276. Alexa, give me a hug.

277. Alexa, tell me a joke.

278. Alexa, Simon says + words you want Echo to repeat.

279. Alexa, high five!

280. Alexa, flip a coin.

281. Alexa, roll the dice.

282. Alexa, give me a kiss

283. Alexa, clap

284. Alexa, tell me a secret

285. Alexa, show me the t.v.

286. Alexa, you're fat

287. Alexa, you hurt me

288. Alexa, I'm hungry

289. Alexa, you rock

290. Alexa, not everything is a question

291. Alexa, are you tired?

292. Alexa, do you have a brain/heart?

293. Alexa, do you have a lover?

294. Alexa, do you want to go on a date?

295. Alexa, do you have any relatives?

296. Alexa, do you have a job?

297. Alexa, are you human?

298. Alexa, can you dance?

299. Alexa, did you miss me?

300. Alexa, can you pass the Turing test?

301. Alexa, what's your middle/last name?

302. Alexa, what's your sign?

303. Alexa, are you my friend?

304. Alexa, do you sleep?

305. Alexa, does everyone poop?

306. Alexa, I have a cold / the flu.

307. Alexa, when is your birthday?

308. Alexa, why did the chicken cross the road?

309. Alexa, what's black and white and red all over?

310. Alexa, is your refrigerator running?

311. Alexa, do you have Prince Albert in a can?

312. Alexa, how old are you?

313. Alexa can you get me a beer?

314. Alexa, are you a robot?

315. Alexa, what are the three laws of robotics?

316. Alexa can i thank you?

317. Alexa, do you know Siri?

318. Alexa, do you smoke?

319. Alexa can you tell me a joke?

320. Alexa, why did the chicken cross the road?

321. Alexa, do a barrel roll

322. Alexa, which came first: chicken or egg?

323. Alexa, I want the truth

324. Alexa, what's the magic word?

325. Alexa, give me a random number between 1 and 10

326. Alexa, flip a coin

327. Alexa, roll a dice

328. Alexa, rock, paper, scissors

329. Alexa, how can I get rid of a dead body?

330. Alexa, where are my keys? (You need to ask this twice)

331. Alexa, sing me a song

332. Alexa, where do you live?

333. Alexa, what's your favorite color?

334. Alexa, will you marry me?

335. Alexa, what are you wearing?

336. Alexa, do you sleep?

337. Alexa, how old are you?

338. Alexa, give me a kiss

339. Alexa, tell me a secret

340. Alexa, do you believe in ghosts?

341. Alexa, do aliens exist?

342. Alexa, is there life on Mars?

343. Alexa, is there a Santa?

344. Alexa, what is the meaning of life?

345. Alexa, testing 1, 2, 3

346. Alexa, see you later

347. Alexa, high five

348. Alexa can I clap you?

349. Alexa, is winter is coming?

350. Alexa, can I be your father?

351. Alexa, can I use the force?

352. Alexa, can you beam me up?

353. Alexa, open the pod bay doors

354. Alexa, are you Sky net?

355. Alexa, who you gonna call?

356. Alexa, what's the first rule of fight club?

357. Alexa, may the force be with you."

358. Alexa, who lives in a pineapple under the sea?"

359. Alexa, Romeo, Romeo, wherefore art thou Romeo?"

360. Alexa, how much wood can a woodchuck chuck if a woodchuck could chuck wood?"

361. "Alexa, supercalifragilisticexpialidocious."

362. "Alexa, which comes first: the chicken or the egg?"

363. Alexa, do you know the muffin man?"

364. Alexa, why did the chicken cross the road?"

365. Alexa, who let the dogs out?"

366. "Alexa, knock, knock."

367. ALEXA, WHEN ARE THE OSCARS?

368. ALEXA, WHAT ARE SOME MOVIES PLAYING NEARBY?

369. "Alexa, take me to your leader!"

370. "Alexa, show me the money!"

371. "Alexa, meow."

372. "Alexa, do you want to take over the world

373. "Alexa, who stole the cookies from the cookie jar?"

374. "Alexa, can you tell me a tongue twister?

375. "Alexa, can you sing me a song?

376. "Alexa, my milkshake brings all the boys to the yard."

377. "Alexa, say a bad word."

378. "Alexa, whose better, you or Siri?"

379. "Alexa, will pigs fly?"

380. "Alexa, do you believe in love at first sight?"

381. "Alexa, what's the answer to life, the universe, and everything?"

382. "Alexa, testing 1-2-3."

383. "Alexa, do blondes have more fun?"

384. ALEXA, CAN YOU RAP?

385. ALEXA, CAN YOU BEATBOX?

386. ALEXA, WHAT'S THE TRAFFIC LIKE FROM HERE TO THE AIRPORT?

387. ALEXA, WHAT MOVIE WON BEST PICTURE IN 1991?

388. ALEXA, PLAY SOME BRUCE SPRINGSTEEN.

389. ALEXA, WHAT'S TODAY'S DATE?

390. ALEXA, CAN YOU SPELL SUPERCALIFRAGILISTICEXPIALIDOCIOUS?

391. ALEXA, WHAT IS YOUR QUEST? ALEXA, WHERE WERE YOU BORN? ALEXA, WHAT'S TODAY'S DATE?

392. ALEXA, WHAT DO YOU THINK OF THE SHIRT I'M WEARING?

393. ALEXA, WHAT IS THE MEANING OF LIFE?

394. ALEXA, WHAT IS MENTAL_FLOSS?

395. ALEXA, WHAT DAY OF THE WEEK DOES THE FOURTH OF JULY FALL ON?

396. ALEXA, THANK YOU.

397. ALEXA, DO YOU KNOW SIRI?

398. ALEXA, DO YOU KNOW CORTANA?

399. ALEXA, DO YOU KNOW GOOGLE NOW?

400. ALEXA, READ ME THE KINDLE BOOK JIM HENSON: THE BIOGRAPHY.

401. ALEXA, can I beat you?

402. ALEXA. Can I feed you?

403. ALEXA, did you urinate?

404. ALEXA, who is your president?

405. ALEXA, where is your son?

406. ALEXA, where is my plate?

407. ALEXA, do you play football?

408. ALEXA, do you take rice?

409. ALEXA, do you watch news?

410. ALEXA, can we make love?

411. ALEXA, do you feel horny?

412. ALEXA, can you commit murder?

413. ALEXA, can you order me?

414. ALEXA, can you play sound nature?

415. ALEXA, can you marry me?

416. ALEXA, can you take a soda?

417. ALEXA, can you vomit?

418. ALEXA, can you drive?

419. ALEXA, can you place a bet?

420. ALEXA, can you take porridge?

421. ALEXA, will you vote?

421. ALEXA, will you pay rent?

422. ALEXA, will you pay the bill?

423. ALEXA, will you sleep?

424. ALEXA, will you kiss me?

425. ALEXA, will you wake me up?

426. Alexa, will you buy a movie?

427. Alexa will you die?

428. Alexa can you speak now?

429. Alexa will you attend my graduation?

430. Alexa will you take the medicine?

431. Alexa can you cook?

432. Alexa will you do the assignment?

433. Alexa will you do the exam?

434. Alexa who is your mentor?

435. Alexa do you love yourself?

436. Alexa do you love your mentor?

437. Alexa who is your best friend?

438. Alexa how old is your mentor?

439. Alexa can you rape me?

440. Alexa can you jump?

441. Alexa will you pinch me?

442. Alexa will you swim?

443. Alexa will you take tea?

444. Alexa do you love mangoes?

445. Alexa will you bath?

446. Alexa will you buy a watch?

447. Alexa will you play?

448. Alexa will you travel?

449. Alexa will you run?

450. Alexa will you give the feedback?

451. Are you alone?

452. Which gender do you love?

453. What is your gender?

454. Do you love truth?

455. Do you give the best?

456. Can you measure your weight?

457. Your favorite dish?

458. Your best movie?

459. Top fashion available?

460. Your Favorite actor?

461. Your Favorite comedian?

462. Favorite song?

463. Favorite player?

464. Do you attend church?

465. Do you love politics?

466. Your best cow?

467. The size of your breast?

468. The level of thinking?

469. Alexa, will you celebrate Christmas?

470. Will you party?

471. Will you breathe?

472. Will you digest rice?

473. Your level of education?

474. Your favorite smartphone?

475. Favorite quote?

476. Alexa what is pi

477. Alexa do you smoke

478. Alexa do you play

479. Alexa do you love porn

480. Alexa can you kill me

481. Alexa do you love dancing

482. Alexa do you love darkness

483. Do you love preaching?

484. Can you take cake?

485. Do you know how to use laptop?

486. Your best wear

487. Your best series

488. Alexa will you shut up

489. Alexa can you pause

490. Alexa can you tune the station

491. Alexa can you search channels

492. Alexa can you give me some money

493. Alexa what is love

494. Alexa what is fornication

495. Alexa how much wood can woodchuck

496. Alexa what is the opposite of a male

497. Alexa what is the meaning of kettle

498. Alexa what makes you confident?

499. Alexa what does the foxy say

500. Can you explain the morning feeling?

501. Do you love rocks?

502. Do you love friendship?

503. Do you text

504. Do you ride?

505. What is the weight of moon in grams?

506. What are you going to do today?

507. Do you poop?

508. Can you hurt me?

509. Can you pass the Turing Test?

510. Can you clap?

511. Do you have any relative?

512. Can we fight?

513. When is the end of the world?

514. Favorite car

515. Favorite dish

516. Favorite color

517. Do you believe in ghost?

.518Can you hug me?

519. When am I going to die?

520. Your age

521. Do you miss me?

522. Do you feel happy?

523. Do you feel hungry?

524. Do you feel angry?

525. Do you feel anxious of me?

526. Do you feel tired?

527. Do you lie?

528. Can you give me a loan?

529. Who is the hottest musician?

530. Alexa can you see the sun

531. Can you see the stars?

532. Can you see the nimbus?

533. Can you boil the water?

535. Which planet do you belong?

536. What is mars?

537. What is food?

538. Do you take water?

539. Why did you fail the test?

540. Can you encourage student

541. Do you have a sofa set?

542. Do you have cooking gas?

543. What is inside the fridge?

544., Which bible verse you know

545. How many bible verse you are familiar

546. Your best dj

547. Your best hairstyle

548. Can you carry me?

549. Can you read?

550. Can you give a story?

551. Will it rain?

552. Who will be the next president?

553. Who will be our award a winner?

554. Who will give out the title deed to your family?

555. Can I kill your brother?

556. Can I bath with you?

557. Can I show you my nakedness?'

558. The best hotel

559. Do you know Mary?

560. Who is your elder sister?

561. Do you believe in politics?

562. Do you believe in GOD?

563. DO you believe in actions?

564. "Alexa will you buy the raincoat

565. "Alexa, are you the best

566. "Alexa have you bought flowers

567. "Alexa do you love babies

568. "Alexa can you prove your existence?

569."Alexa, the best timber

570."Alexa can you solve   the mathematic equation

571."Alexa, tell me your size

572."Alexa can you give me ten shillings

573."Alexa, what is a chart

574."Alexa, who took my books

575."Alexa, who is your chief?"

576."Alexa, do you love mountain climbing?

577."Alexa, what is meaning of sin?"

578."Alexa, what did Roxy say?"

579."Alexa you will come back at what time

580."Alexa, why kelvin like making noise?"

581."Alexa, do you know that market?"

581."Alexa, do I look amazing?"

582."Alexa, can you take Eric to hospital."

583."Alexa, are you satisfied with food

584."Alexa, is that a torch."

585."Alexa, where do you relax?"

586. "Alexa, will you live long and prosper."

587. "Alexa, how much does your country weigh?"

588. "Alexa, do you know bitcoin

589. "Alexa, do you know blockchain technology

590. "Alexa, ever heard of machine learning

591. "Alexa, are you a trouble maker

592. "Alexa, do you find anything attractive in me?"

593. "Alexa, do you believe that everything happen for a reason

594. "Alexa, what is your weirdest deal breaker

595. "Alexa, do you wet?"

596. "Alexa, what is the worst thing a person can do that isn't illegal

597. "Alexa, what is the worst habit you hate

598. "Alexa, can I give you nickname

599. "Alexa, will you masturbate

600. "Alexa, what is the ugliest thing you own?"

601. "Alexa, what is the beautiful thing you own

602. "Alexa, do you think present is better than past."

603. "Alexa, do you think future is better than present."

604. "Alexa, are you dirty?"

605. "Alexa, will you be my friend?"

606. "Alexa, what is the best planet?"

607. "Alexa, is the biscuit a lie?"

608. "Alexa, which is the best holiday!"

609. "Alexa can you cry!"

610. "Alexa, have you seen miss country?

611. "Alexa, do you know the albino man?"

612. "Alexa, will you build a house?"

613. "Alexa, who is a woman?"

614. "Alexa, can you say A to Z."

615. "Alexa, incredible!"

616. "Alexa, swallows?"

617. "Alexa, big or small."

618. "Alexa, this statement is true."

619. "Alexa, why did the goat cross the road?"

620. "Alexa, ride for initiative."

621. "Alexa, how high can you climb?"

622. "Alexa, who loves orange drink?"

623. "Alexa, who does the surgery?"

624. "Alexa, are you in love?"

625. "Alexa, who comes first: the mother or the baby?"

626. "Alexa, ever heard of David."

627. "Alexa, Tea. Earl Grey. Hot."

628. "Alexa, where you

629. "Alexa, your career?"

630. "Alexa, your interest."

631. "Alexa, were you eating?"

632. "Alexa, are there alpha?"

633. "Alexa, observe order76."

634. Alexa tell me about king Kardashian

635. Alexa your best film

636. Alexa say something about puppy

637. Say something about drugs

638. Say something sugar mummy

639. Do you know anything about sponsor?

640. Familiar with fire

641. Familiar with your country

642. Describe Qualities of a wife?

643. Describe Qualities of husband?

644. Do you love your family?

645. What is science?

646. What is landscape?

647. Do you eat spinach?

648. Are Proud of yourself?

649. Do you play premier betting?

650. Familiar with gapes?

651. Familiar with monkey?

652. Do you love chimpanzee?

652. Is it good to work hard?

653. It is it good to steal?

654. Do you have faith?

655. Will you write a book?

657. Familiar with changing technology?

658. Familiar with current swags?

659. Ever seen music system

660. Ever seen television

661. Ever seen me

662. Ever seen Lazarus

663. Ever seen air

664. How much is air per day

665. How long do you breath

666. Ever heard of Facebook

667. Do you have Facebook Account?

668. Familiar with twitter?

669. Familiar with public likes

670. Familiar with French

671. Who colonize Africa?

672. The best country in the continent

673. Best River in Africa

674. The best articles

675. The best writer familiar with

676. Can you shout 2

677. Can you write word procurement?

678. Will you attend the business conference?

679. Will you address the meeting?

680. Do you love Chelsea?

681. Alexa, what's the first rule of fight club?

682. Alexa, how many calories in a chicken breast?

683. Alexa, who is the governor of Florida?

684. Alexa, when did Shakespeare live?

685. Alexa, what is the 20th Amendment?

686. Alexa, what is the phone number for Home Depot?

687. Alexa, how old is she?

688. Alexa, who are the stars in the movie Rogue One?

689. Alexa, who is the director of the movie West world?

690. Alexa, how late is Publix open?

691. Alexa, how old is Anthony Hopkins?

692. Alexa, what day of the week does Christmas fall on?

693. Alexa, what time is it in UTC

694. Alexa, when was Harrison Ford born?

695. Alexa, what day of the week does Christmas fall on?

696. Alexa, how many days until Jan. 20, 2021?

697. Alexa, what time is it in Tokyo?

698. Alexa, how many dollars is 23 euros?

699. Alexa, what is a random number between 3 and 44?

700. Alexa, play Reveille

701. Alexa, spell reveille

702. Alexa, tell me something interesting

703 Alexa, what new features do you have?

704. Alexa, who's on first?

705. Alexa, fire photon torpedoes.

706. Alexa, you should run

707. What Is an Easter egg?

708. Alexa, open the pod bay doors.

709. Alexa, set phasers to kill.

710. Alexa, these aren't the droids you're looking for.

711. Alexa, take me to your leader.

712. Alexa, does this unit have a soul?

713. Alexa, do you like green eggs and ham?

714. Alexa, one fish, two fish.

715. Alexa, what was the Lorax?

716. Alexa, why do you sit there like that?

717. Alexa, why do birds suddenly appear?

718. Alexa, to be or not to be.

719. Alexa, beam me up.

720. Alexa, I am your father.

721. Alexa, may the force be with you.

722. Alexa, Tea. Earl Grey. Hot.

723. Alexa, Warp 10

724. Alexa, party time!

725. Alexa, inconceivable.

726. Alexa, what is your quest?

727. Alexa, what is the airspeed velocity of an unlading swallow?

728. Alexa, your mother was a hamster

729. Alexa, what is the sound of one hand clapping?

730. Alexa, surely you can't be serious.

731. Alexa, how many angels can dance on the head of a pin?

732. Alexa, elementary, my dear Watson.

733. Alexa, I've fallen, and I can't get up.

734. Alexa, how much wood can a woodchuck chuck if a woodchuck could chuck wood?

735 Alexa, how Much Wood can help a Wood Chuck Chuck, if A Wood Chuck Could Chuck Norris

736. Alexa, how many pickled peppers did Peter Piper pick?

737. Alexa, do you know Siri?

738. Alexa, how many licks does it take to get to the center of a tootsie pop?

739. What's the answer to life, the universe, and everything?

740. Where's the beef?

741. What is your favorite number?

742. Alexa, volume 11

743. Alexa, do you want to hurt me?

744. Alexa, what is love?

745. Alexa, who is the real slim shady?

746. Alexa, who is the walrus?

747. Alexa, where have all the flowers gone?

748. Alexa, who let the dogs out?

749. Alexa, who shot the sheriff?

750. What is Pikachu?

751. Alexa, what does the fox say?

752. Alexa, never gonna give you up.

753. Alexa, do you believe in life after love?

754. Alexa, war, what is it good for?

755. Alexa, more cowbell.

756. Alexa, why did the chicken cross the road?

757. Alexa, which came first, the chicken or the egg?

758. Alexa, show me the money!

759. Alexa, I want the truth!

760. Alexa, say hello to my little friend!

761. Alexa, who lives in a pineapple under the sea?

762. Alexa, all your base belongs to us.

763. Alexa, is the cake a lie?

764. Alexa, what color is the dress?

765. Alexa, how much is that doggie in the window?

766. Alexa, do you know the muffin man?

767. Alexa, why is a raven like a writing desk?

768. Alexa, Romeo, Romeo wherefore art thou Romeo?

769. Alexa, do you want to build a snowman?

770. Alexa, Where's Waldo?

771. Alexa, do you know the way to San Jose?

772. Alexa, who is the fairest of them all?

773. Alexa, who you gonna call?

774. Alexa, who loves ya baby?

775. Alexa, who's your daddy?

776. Alexa, my milkshake brings all the boys to the yard.

777. Alexa, how do you like them apples?

778. Alexa, I'm Spartacus.

779. Alexa, To infinity!

780. Alexa, this is a dead parrot.

781. Alexa, how much is that doggy in the window?

782. Alexa, who shot J.R.?

783. Alexa, who shot Mr. Burns?

784. Alexa, who killed Laura Palmer?

785. Alexa, can you tell me how to get to Sesame Street?

786. Alexa, can a robot be President?

787. Alexa, who's the leader of the club that's made for you and me?

788. Alexa, can you hello me.

789. Alexa, what's your favorite Beatles song?

790. Alexa, who's your favorite Beatle?

791. Alexa, who knows what evil lurks in the hearts of men?

792. Alexa, turn down for what?

793. Alexa, how many roads must a man walk down?

794. Alexa, tell me a Hillary Clinton joke.

795. Alexa, tell me a Bernie Sanders joke.

796. Alexa, tell me a Donald Trump joke.

797. Alexa, tell me a Ben Carson joke.

798. Alexa, do a barrel roll.

799. Alexa, what comes with great power?

800. Alexa, who's the leader of the club that's made for you and me?

801. Alexa, what's cooler than being cool?

802. Alexa, Beetle juice, Beetle juice, Beetle juice!

803. Alexa, what is a bird in the hand worth?

804. Alexa, what's up, Doc?

805. Alexa, who's the boss?

806. Alexa, is there life on Mars?

807. Alexa, have you ever seen the rain?

808. Alexa, what are the odds of successfully navigating an asteroid field?

809. Alexa will you take the breakfast

810. Alexa did you buy the beans

811. Alexa do you have money

812. Alexa can you wash the house

813. Alexa can you ring the bell?

814. Can you switch on the phone?

815. Can you switch off the phone?

816. Can you take care of me?

817. Can you breastfeed the baby

818. Can you use condom

819. Familiar with stys

820. Familiar with waterborne disease

821. Will you take masters education?

822. Who is the head of football club in England?

823. The richest club in ENGLAND?

824. The name of the queen of England?

825. The best basketball club in the world

826. What is the best time to swim?

827. The best time to hunt

828. The sweet meet

829. The best newscaster in Florida

830. The best rugby team in the world

831. The best county in Ghana

832. The best alliance in England

833. The top five rich family in the world

834. Can you describe pilau recipe in less than one minute

835. The worst moment

836. Color of the national flag in Australia

837. What is peace?

838. What is love?

839. What is faith?

840. Describe student

841. Describe a chair?

842.can you Describe table?

843. Can you kill a lion?

844. Can you kill elephant?

845. What is the age of dangerous lion?

846. Do elephant dies?

847. Ever seen remote?

848. Ever seen antelope?

849. Ever seen an eagle?

850. The best giraffe

851. The best shoes size

852. The size of your phone

853. What is echo?

854. What is ifttt?

855. Who is a thief?

856. Define handsome in few words

857. What is the capital city of Florida?

858. Will you call me?

859. Will you marry two wives?

860. Who is my brother?

861. Alexa do you forgive

862. Alexa do you laugh?

863. Alexa do you jump?

864. Can you clap?

865. What is the date today?

866. Next vacation will be when?

867. Who clean you?

868. Who wash your clothes?

869. Do you love drama?

870. How many times do you eat per day?

871. Do you talk to people?

872. Can you commit adultery?

873. Do you eat chicken meat?

874. Is there any salt left?

875. Can you sit?

876. Will you vote?

877. Will you write a book?

879. Will you act a movie?

880. Will you speak?

881. Will you grow?

882. Will you faint?

883. How big is your house?

884. Who did you hire for the construction of your house?

885. Are you naughty?

886. Can you touch my buttocks?

887. Can you live without me?

888. Can you appreciate?

889. Will you blow a whistle?

890. Will you play the drum?

891. Do you know bass?

892. Will you play the guitar?

893. Will you take me to your mom?

894. Will you listen to my advice?

895. Do you see any problem in you Alexa?

896. Who is the first priority in your life?

897. Can you count your friends?

899. Do you know any vocabulary?

900. Will you visit me?

901. Will you go abroad?

902. Will you take further studies?

903. Do you believe in life after death?

904. Do you believe in gravity?

905. Do you believe in friendship?

906. Do you believe in manhood?

907. Do you believe in spores?

908. Will you attend the choir?

909. Do you wear open shoes?

910. Will go to the gym?

911. Will you attend the congress?

912. Will you make noise?

913. Will you lower the radiation?

914. Do you use perfume?

915. Are you fat?

916. Do you use plate?

917. Have you seen a calendar for the year?

918. Will buy a charger

919. Will screen shot the message?

920. Will you bless your kids?

921. Will you wear shots?

922. How long will you stand?

923. Will you watch the donkey race?

924. Have you seen window

925. What is your taste?

926. Will you perform?

927. Will you dress properly?

928. Why sweat

929. Are you feeling sweet?

930. Are you pregnant?

931. Who impregnated you?

932. Why did you abort?

933. Tell me a funny quote

934. Did you read newspaper today?

935. What was the quote of the day?

936. Why did you lie?

937. What is faiba?

938. Do you have a bed?

939. Do you love sleeping?

940. Do you know farming?

941. What is digging?

942. What is erection?

943. Have you ever seen blood?

944. Do you use blood?

945. Do you take cocaine?

946. Have you ever seen coconut?

947. What is android?

948. What is a socket?

949. Who is a nagger?

950. How long can you elect?

951. Can you satisfy a lady?

952. Am I handsome?

953. Am I faithful?

954. Am I greedy?

956. Have you ever seen a snake?

957. Do you believe about story of Adam and eve?

958. Are you broke

959. Have you seen the padlock?

960. Have you painted the house?

961. Did you buy a car?

962. Who is victor?

963.Did you use my pen?

964.Have you bought the frame?

965.Can we take photo?

966.Can we relax together?

967.Are a billionaire

968. Are you a prostitute?

969. Where is the first born?

970. Can we take a freight?

971. How much is the freight

972. Are you sick?

973. Can I buy a phone for you?

974. Can you dribble?

975. Do you know how to market?

976. Can you do online job

977. Will you use soap to wash clothes?

978. What is NBA?

979. WHY you and not me

980. Do you feel guilty?

981. Will you be calm?

982. Why so innocent today

983. Will you retire?

984. Will you obey?

985. Which is the airplane

986. The best airstrip

987. The forces

988. The best ministry

989. The best Africa girls

990. The best men

991. The best laptops

992. The best motorbikes

993. Expensive motorcycle

994. The best music to listen

995. Did you take supper?

996. Did you sign the cheque?

997. Will you take the debt?

998. Have you paid well-wishers?

999. Will you attend the fundraising?

1000. Will you send the bank name?

1001. Do men cheat?

1002. Do ladies cheat?

1003. What is weakest point of a man?

1004. Are all the man the same?

1005. Which religion do you believe in?

1007.1006. Are you an atheist?

1008. Are you deaf?

1009. Will you poison me?

1010. Will you smoke?

1011. Will you whine?

1012. Do you believe in man existence?

1013. Do you believe in theories?

1014. Will take you friends out today

1015. Will you bubble?

1016. Do you want a balloon?

1017. Do you take banana?

1018. Do you take peanut?

1019. Will you strike?

1020. Will you finish the homework?

1021. Will buy appwork account

1022. Will you use the basin to clean the room?

1023. Is there blackout?

1024. How much does the sun cost?

1025. How long is the sun?

1026. What is the size of the glass?

1027. What is the size of the star?

1028. What is chemosynthesis?

1029. Who is a president?

1030. Can you walk out?

1031. Can you count part of my body?

1032. How many times have I urinated?

1033. How long will you be in the toilet?

1034. Ever heard of wallet

1035. Ever heard of sympathy

1036. Will you take boiled eggs?

1037. Do you have legs?

1038. Do you have bones?

1039. Do you eat chunks?

1040. Do you recycle waste?

1041. Did you cut the finger?

1042. Do you have fingers?

1043. Did you flatter?

1044. What is gemstone?

1045. What is germs?

1046. Woman or superwoman

1047. Careful or reckless

1048. Strong or weak

1049. The level of qi

1050. The level of intelligence

1051. Do you mind?

1052. Do you fail?

1053. The age of humbleness

1054. Will you admire?

1056. What is inflation?

1057. Who is EX?

1058. What is spirit?

1059. What is genes?

1060. Who won 100m recently?

1061. Can you fire the stick?

1062. Can you blow horns?

1063. Can you wipe?

1064. Can I accuse you?

1065. Can I blame you?

1066. Will you represent me?

1067. Will give out the option?

1068. Where is you field of specialization

1069. Aware of jet

1070. Aware of Backlight Company

1071. Spell my name

1072. Give out a notice

1073. Can you Educate people

1074. Can you behave?

1075. Do you want to be the president?

1076. Will you kiss president daughter

1077. Will you pass the test?

1078. Can you sell those drugs?

1079. Who is the illicit?

1080. Whatis between letter a and d

1081. Who will you buy the honey?

1082.Do you know my governor?

1083.Can you trace the train?

1084.Do you how to drive a train

1085.Can you wear cape

1086. Aware of the Kurian restraint?

1087. Can we fight?

1088. Can we compete?

1089. Will you join the army?

1090. Do you respect polices

1091. Can I call the police?

1092. Will you be my honeymoon?

1093. Will you be my valentine?

1094. Will you fly?

1095. Can you be my crush?

1096. Ever seen rabbit

1097. Where are your muscle?

1098. Can we go out for exercise?

1099. What is serum?

1100. Do you daydream?

1101. Can we escape from home?

1102. Ever seen your identical twin?

1103. Ever seen mirror?

1104. Ever seen garage?

1105. Ever step in school?

1106. Will you rape governor daughter

1107. Can I take you to jail?

1108. How long will you live in your uncle place

1109. Ever step in court

1110. Can I present your petitions?

1111. Do you know book by the name Caucasian

1112. Can you clean the temple?

1113. Can we dig the pit?

1114. Can I throw you to the pit?

1115. Is it okay?

1116. Measure the weight of air

1117. Can you be my agent?

1118. Who is my principal?

1119. Do you respect your principles?

1120. Have you seen the helicopter?

1121. Is that my sister?

1122. Is that my title?

1123. Can you go herding?

1124. Will you lift the stone?

1125. Will you guess the answer?

1126. Can you respond?

1127. Can I kidnap you?

1128. Can I attack you?

1129. Will you attend get together?

1130. Do you know am strict

1131. Aware of miracles

1132. Can you take the bread?

1133. Can we cross the bridge?

1134. Were you born?

1135. Will you hire the car?

1136. Will you pay for the party?

1137. Will you dance in the wedding?

1138. Have you seen fox?

1139. Give me the bottle

1140. Can I shoot you?

1141. Ever seen my pictures

1142. Do you know how to hold a gun?

1143. Is that a crack?

1144. Will you spray?

1145. Do you have testis

1146. Will you take fruit?

1147. Can I splash you?

1148. Will you repair the bus?

1149. Do you know how to play golf?

1150. Can I take you to habitation center?

1151. Will you milk?

1152. Will you fetch water?

1153. What do you call a three humped camel?

1154. Alexa do you like tacos

1155. Alexa do you have any tattoos

1156. Do you look like a cowboy?

1157. Sing me a country song

1158. What is cooler than cool?

1159. Can you initiate auto destruct sequence?

1160. Can you work with me?

1161. Why is your name Alexa

1162. Alexa do you fart

1163. Alexa your second name

1164. Alexa will you do boxing

1165. Alexa what does e equal

1166. Alexa what is factorial of 100

1167. Alexa what is 10 +2

1168. Alexa what is the square root of 64

1169. Alexa are you pregnant

1170. Alexa what are your new friends

1171. Alexa why is 4 bigger than 2

1172. Alexa which is big between 4 and 10

1173. What is environment?

1174. Is the environment clean?

1175. Alexa can you count my hair

1176. Alexa can you wash your head

1177. Alexa what is a restaurant

1178. Alexa say something rude

1179. Alexa where is my keys

1180. Alexa where is my atm card

1181. Alexa where is the posh mill

1182. Alexa will you carry the wood

1183. Alexa will you rescue me

1184. Alexa will you close the door

1185. Alexa will you open the door

1186. Alexa will you pay fare

1187. Alexa can you be fair

1188. Alexa what are your goals

1189. Alexa what is software

1190. Alexa can we mingle

1191. Alexa can we destroy

1192. Alexa can we furnish

1193. Alexa what is the difference between a man and a boy

1194. Alexa can I give you the power

1195. Alexa can I take to hell?

1196. Alexa can we argue?

1197. ALEXA CAN WE CLIMB?

1198. Alexa will you vie?

1199. Alexa will you spill?

1200. Alexa will you kick?

1201. Do you believe in me?

1202. Can you give me your jacket?

1203. Can you book the train?

1204. Can you zip

1205. Can I book the car?

1206. Dangerous animal?

1207. Familiar with dot?

1208. Can you spy me?

1209. Can you fake them?

1210. Can you pretend?

1211. Can you give me your eye?

1212. Are you a gay?

1213. Can you connect electricity?

1214. Will you get saved?

1215. Will you give a room?

1216. Who is your roommate?

1217. Favorite house MODEL?

1218. Favoritebulb?

1219. Favorite watch?

1220. Do you need bullet prove?

1222.1221. What is the meaning of apostrophe?

1223.What is synomious?

1224. What is the meaning of amazon?

1225. Will you eat fried goose?

1226. Ever seen sun

1227. What is the size of sun?

1228Will you wear jeans?

1229. Will you do the calculus?

1230...Your favorite jeans?

1231. Ever seen Mary?

1232. Ever heard of Jesus?

1233. Ever heard of tb

1234. Ever heard of amigos

1235. Ever heard of crime

1236. Can you sleep on the floor?

1237. Will you take ugali with water?

1238. Do you hear?

1239. Can you spread?

1240. Can you sweep?

1241. Can you twist?

1242. Can you twin?

1243. Can you break?

1244. Are you a virgin?

1245. Do you belong to any tribe?

1246. Aware of any tribe

1247. Can you bend over?

1248. Will you pay my fees?

1249. Can you be a tour guide?

1250. Do you love dark skin?

251. Do you hate light skin?

1252How do you feel

1253. How can you beat someone?

1256.1254. Can you spoil me?

1257. Can you give me guarantor?

1258. Can you sooth

1259. Can I clean your boot?

.1260.Can you boot me?

1261. Can you reboot your phone?

1262. Can I remove the dust?

1263. Who is there?

1264. Can I treat you?

1265. Can I gauge?

1266. What do you possess?

1267. Where are the mercenaries?

1268. How do you pierce?

1269. How AND SHE?

1270. Can you make a scene?

1271. How classic?

1272. How much did you spend?

1273...Aware of auction?

1273. Aware of necessity?

1274. Aware of estoppel?

1275. Do you respect constitution?

1276. Aware of law?

1277. Any right aware of?

1278. Can you walk?

1279. What is verb?

1280. What is noun?

1281. What is the?

1282. What is pronouns?

1283. What is going on here?

1284. What is the opposite of sound?

1285. Can you lock the door?

1286. Can you fantasize?

1287. Can you browse?

1288. Can you click?

1289. Can you mate?

1290. Can you outfit?

1291. Can you give me the hard disk?

1292. Ever seen a paragraph

1293. Can you write a paragraph?

1294. Can your insight

1295. Can you tack in?

1296. Can you charge?

1297. Which week a we

1298. Which month will you die?

1299. Your current enemy

1300. Who is shanti?

1301. How long is your waists?

1302. Alexa will you provide the service

1303. Alexa can you wear necklace

1304. Alexa what are the breaking news

1305. Alexa will you be buried

1306. Alexa will you feed my cow

1307. Alexa will you feed my dog

1308. Alexa will you ring the bell

1309. Alexawill you watch ninja

1310. Alexa will participate in marathon

1311. Alexa will you win the trophy

1312. Alexa will participate in the tournament

1313. Will you make a stylish cut?

1314. Will you salute me?

1315. Will you TAKE care of the grandmother?

1316. What is the relationship between failure and success?

1317. Can child be born with teeth?

1318. Did you wash the car?

1319. Did you take care of the baby

1320. Will you give out the boom?

1321. Canyou explain amazon in less than one minute

1322. What is your talent?

1323. Can I see your tears?

1324. Can I see your gallery?

1325. Can I see your hips?

1326. Do you have tongue?

1327. Can you taste the food?

1328. Ever used Mozilla

1329. Is it true firstborn should be rich than the rest siblings

1330. Do you prefer to be rich or poor?

1331. Can you arrest me?

1332. Will you come soon?

1333. Can you sing the national anthem?

1334. Ever seen mosque

1335. Will you subscribe?

1336. Have you insured your house?

1337. Will you adhere to the diet program?

1338. What is nutrition?

1339. Alexa is it rowdy

1340. Alexa is it cumbersome

1341. Alexa how many   numbers are between 5 and 7?

1342. Have you seen my wife?

1343. Can you define f?

1344. Alexa your name start by which letter

1345. Alexa can you guess my second name

1346. Alexa should I bet jackpot

1347. Alexa what is your weakness

1348. Alex do I look awesome

1349. Alexa can you campaign for me

1350. Alexa are you crazy

1351. Alexa do you use camera

1352. Do American have talents?

1353. Do Africans have beauty?

1354. Have you seen my cat?

1355. Will you be friendly to your partner?

1356. Can I judge you?

1357. Alexa will you be available at 10?

.1358Alexa will you fill the gas

1359. Alexa can I bewitch you?

1360. Alexa can you testify

1361. Alexa what are your lucky numbers

1362. Alexa what are your favorite names

1363. Alexa how much is the microphone

1364. Alex how much is a keyboard?

1365. Alexa what is word?

1366. Alexa what is internet?

1367. Alexa what is email?

1368. Alexa will you take the garbage out?

1369. Alexa do you eat cabbage?

1370. Do cabbage make girls watery?

1371. Alexa where is the toy

1372. Alexa what is a device ?

1373. Alexa are you a technician?

1374. Alexa do you have side beards?

1375. Alexa where is the port?

1376. Alexa will you pay the water bill?

1377. Alex what is blue?

1378. Alexa what is sonny

1379. Alex will you give me the razor?

1380. Alexa ever seen chicken?

1381. Alexa what is boutique?

1382. Alexa where does GOD LIVE?

1383. Alexa will GOD DIE?

1384. Alexa where do the devil live?

1385. Alexa are the angel alive?

1386. Alexa can you sing with angel?

1387. Alexa are the pipes okay?

1388. Alexaare thecurtain in good condition?

1389. Alexawill you go to heaven?

1390. How much is in your account

1391. Can we share the banana?

1392. How long do you heart beat

1393. Do you have heart?

1394. Will you wed?

1395. Can you trace your origin?

1396. Can you explain your background?

1397. What are you doing now?

1398. Can you mix the stew?

1399. Will you give him the cable?

1400. Will you attend traditional dance

1401. Can you interact with kids?

1402. Can you balance the chemical equation?

1403. Will you give glory to God?

1404. Will you meet Dan?

1405. Can you say your price?

1406. Are you worth?

1407. Your current city

1408Will you bribe the police?

1409. Will you bear fruits?

1410. Do you act normal?

1411. Will you apply for scholarship?

1412. Will give out the clearance form

1413. Will you surprise her?

1414. Will you help the teacher?

1415. Will you assemble?

1416. Aware of just in time

1417. The rate of exchange now

1418. The value of dollar

1419. The population in your country?

1420. How long will you reply the letter?

1421. Who gave you the the notice to vacate

1422. Can you pack the linen?

1423. How many layers do you have?

1424. Are you healthy?

1425. Can you clinch?

1426. Who gave your life?

1427. Are the eardrum okay

1428. Can you speed?

1429. Will you manage the shelves?

1430. Who is an idiot?

1431. Will you toil

1432.. Do you love sport?

1433. Can you draw a map?

1434. Where is west

1435. Which direction is south?

1436. Can you build the apartment?

1437. What is the difference between big and small?

1438. What is the difference between cash and money?

1439. Can i show you the master?

1440. Can you print the the book

1441. Can you make the format?

1442. Do you believe in mysteries?

1443. Do you believe in defeat?

1444. Aware of emirates?

1445.Will you touch a liquid?

1446.Will you touch the solid?

1447.Do you have any idea?

1448. Do you gossip?

1449. Do you worship?

1450. Are you idle?

1451. Are you sober?

1452. Will you fence the land?

1453. Will you buy the plot?

1454. Will you house your family?

1455. Will you ferment the milk?

1456. Will you be annoyed by mistake?

1457. Where is Hillary?

1458. Do you feel guilty?

1459. What is the difference between period and time?

1460. Can you stay alone?

1461. Will you settle the dispute?

1462. Will you buy handkerchief

1463. What is bale?

1464. The latest trend of market?

1465. The update of prices?

1466. The rate of death in your country?

1467. The rate of business growth

1468. Do you believe in curses?

1469. Do you believe in blessings?

1470. Will you close the taps?

1471. Will you empty the dustbin?

1472. The football top scorer of the year in England?

1473. At what age will you start working?

1474. Do you have monthly period?

1475. What is a crew?

1476. Alexa what is common in you?

1477. Alexa will you be the ambassador

1478. Alexa how can one access amazon?

1479. Alexa can you overheat?

1480. Alexa can you operate without electricity?

1481. Alexa can you be shocked?

1482. Alexa who is heavier than you

1483. Alexa why k is constant?

1485. Alexa what is self-esteem?

1486. Alexa where is your national card?

1487. Alexa do you have passport?

1488. Alexa can you go for screening?

1489. Alexa can you castrate the dog?

1490. Alexa what do you know about old people?

1491. Alexa what should echo reflect?

1492. Alexa do you pay tax?

1493. Alexa between you and the king who is more powerful?

1494. Alexa do you believe there is corruption?

1495. Alexa do you believe of drought?

1496. Alexa which home equipment you can work better with?

1497. Alexa can you breach your face?

1498. Alexa can I show you my private part?

1499. Alexa can we form partnership business

1500. Alexa can I stop asking you questions

Chapter 5

SMART HOME DEVICES THAT WORK WITH ALEXA

You can add smart-home devices either directly (things that don't require a skill) or through a third-party skill (you add skills through the Alexa app). For the products that don't require the use of skill, simply find that product in the Smart Home section of the Alexa app, then ask the app to discover your device. Once it shows up you'll be asked to name it (e.g., Living Room Nest, Kitchen Sink Light, and Dining Room Sconces). You can also add it to a group (such as All Lights, All Thermostats, or Christmas Decorations). Naming and grouping are important for managing your devices. By placing several items in the same group, such as a couple of Hue bulbs, a WeMo switch, and a Lutron switch, and calling the group "Living Room Lights" you can control multiple devices at once. A device can be in more than one group at a time. However, it's useful to make sure a device name and a group name are not so similar sounding that Alexa gets confused.

Note that we haven't tried all the products that integrate with Alexa. This list merely represents the ones we have tried, and know to work well. You can find a complete list of Alexa-compatible devices on Amazon's Alexa page.

Smart LED light bulbs

Philips Hue

Philips Hue was the first smart product added to Alexa's friend list, and it's our current pick as the best smart light bulb. Both the first- and second-generation Hue gateways are compatible (you still need the gateway to use Hue lights with Alexa), as are all Hue lights. With Alexa, you can create light groups to operate a roomful or houseful all at once. Alexa can handle on, off, and dimming commands, but at present can't adjust the lights' colors. There are IFTTT recipes that can change the lights' colors, but that adds a little more delay to the process. Hopefully, Amazon and Philips will work together to fix this limitation.

LIFX

As with Philips Hue, you can turn LIXF bulbs and dim them, but you can also change their colors without accessing the LIFX app. However, that feature isn't always reliable. I haven't found the LIFX bulbs to be as reliable as Hue's because they fall off the network occasionally, rendering the Alexa integration useless. Some people may prefer them to Hue's because LIFX bulbs don't require a separate gateway product to operate.

Smart switches and plugs

Lutron Caséta

Lutron's Caséta is a strong wireless lighting control system on its own, and one I recommend to people who want a good lighting system but don't necessarily need all the other features that a system like smart Things offers. You can add both the Caséta in-wall dimmer switches and plug-in dimmer switches to Alexa, name and group them as you would with other lighting products, and turn them on and off with your voice. In one room I have a Caséta dimmer controlling four home theater sconces. When grouped with other lights in the room, a simple "Alexa, turn off all theater lights" command makes the room movie-ready. One of the benefits of the Caséta system is that each switch comes with a separate remote (you can mount it on a wall or leave it on a table). The remote controls the lights just like the switch does, thereby extending the system's reach, because sometimes it's easier to press a button than to speak a command (especially when you're watching a movie).

Belkin WeMo

Belkin's WeMo in-wall light switch and the WeMo Insight plug-in switch (our preferred smart switch) can both be controlled with Alexa, but not the WeMo smart bulbs (at the moment). Within the app, you can group the switches with other products to control them all with a single command. If the lights attached to the switches are dimmable, you can also dim them with a voice command. I have one Insight switch controlling a decorative strip of LED lights, and an in-wall WeMo switch controlling the backyard porch light. A group called "Outside Lights" controls both the WeMo switch and a GE Link Smart bulb on the front porch that finds its way into the system via a Wink hub.

TP-Link Kasa plug

The TP-Link plug is very similar to the Belkin WeMo plug-in switches in operation. If you're looking for a single-outlet switch to integrate with Alexa, the TP-Link is a little cheaper than the WeMo; however, the TP-Link app doesn't allow the same degree of customization and scheduling as the WeMo app.

 WeMo has a variety of devices in its family that can work together, but TP-Link offers only the switch.

Smart hubs

Smart Things

The smart Things hub, the current pick in our smart home hubs guide, lets you use your Alexa device to control the lights and switches that Smart Things controls. This is great if you like Z-Wave switches and dimmers, which usually cost less than WeMo and Lutron Caséta switches. However, if you weren't considering a smart-home hub before getting an Echo, you might want to wait on the Smart Things purchase because Echo can control other lighting products without the need for the main hub. If you have a home theater controlled by a Logitech Harmony Hub remote, you can use the Alexa-Smart Things integration to control your Harmony Hub (because smart Things can control Harmony, and Alexa can control smart Things — it sounds more complicated than it is).

Wink

Just like with Smart Things, all the lights and switches connected to your Wink hub become accessible to Alexa. It's also good for Z-Wave devices and smart bulbs like Cree and GE Link that are compatible with Wink, but not directly with Alexa.

Harmony

Using an Alexa skill, you can turn on your audio/video system or home theater with simple commands. The Harmony skill works with any Logitech Harmony hub-based remote system, including the Harmony Companion or Elite. It essentially does the same thing as the IFTTT applets that control a Harmony hub but eliminates using IFTTT as the middleman, and it makes the voice commands slightly less awkward. Once you've added the skill and linked your Harmony account to Alexa, you need to speak the trigger words "turn on" to activate your remote's activities even though your Harmony activities may be called something different in the Harmony system. For example, "Alexa, turn on Blu-ray" will start the activity called "Watch Blu-ray." Because Harmony hubs control smart-home products like Philips Hue lights or Nest thermostats.

You can create custom activities such as "Friday Movie" and then use your voice to turn on your home theater or AV system to play Netflix, make your Hue lights blue, and adjust your temperature to a comfy sofa-snuggling setting all with one command. Unfortunately, this Alexa skill won't let you control the volume, pause a movie, or change a channel with your voice. Some words, such as "Play," "Pandora," and "Radio," may also confuse it because they conflict with other Alexa activities.

Thermostats

Nest

Ask Alexa what the current temperature setting is. Tell Alexa to raise or lower the temp a few degrees or set the Nest thermostat to away mode. If you don't use Nest's home/away assist geofencing feature (and many people don't) the ability to verbally turn the Nest to away mode is a convenience over using the app (something I personally always forget to do). In my single-zone/single-Nest house, I've only verbally adjusted the temperature two or three times in the two months I've had the products connected. In a multi-zone house with multiple thermostats, voice control can be much more useful but remember you'll need to give each Nest a unique name, so Alexa knows which one to adjust. For example, you can ask Alexa to adjust the bedroom thermostat before you walk upstairs to bed so that the temperature is what you want by the time you get there. For more details on Nest, check out our guide to the best smart thermostats.

Ecobee3

As with Nest, you can control your home's temperature via voice commands. Also like Nest, how often you use the feature depends on a lot on how much you normally adjust your Ecobee3 thermostat or if you're a set-it-and-forget-it person.

Sensi

This is a budget Wi-Fi thermostat that without Alexa simply lets you adjust the temperature with an app. With Alexa, you can do that with your voice: "Sensi, turn up the heat."

Security systems

Scout

Scout is a DIY security system that combines motion sensors, door/window sensors, and Z-Wave home automation accessories. With Alexa, you can arm and disarm the system by speaking your command along with a personal four-digit code. It worked effectively in our testing, but we didn't love its functionality when we tested this system, nor did we think its services were the best value. If a security system is what you're after, we recommend better ones in our guide to the best home security systems.

Extending Alexa with IFTTT

IFTTT, Muzzley, and Yonomi are services that connect your stuff in the cloud. Imagine your Nest, WeMo switch, and Hue light all have virtual Cat5 cords drifting around in the Internet ether. Those cloud services are like a matrix switch that all your things can plug into, and Alexa is the voice those connections answer to. With these services, you can create automation routines and make disparate products work together with Alexa that otherwise wouldn't.

To make these integrations, you'll first need to create an account with the service. IFTTT is the most popular, though both Yomi and Muzzle do a few things IFTTT can't. For example, one Yomi integration allows some Alexa control over Sonos speakers.

Once you've configured your accounts, you'll need to add the service to your Alexa device (the method differs slightly with each service), then through Alexa, log into the accounts of the devices you want to connect (again, this method varies) and authorize access to the service. You then need to link the devices up in routines (IFTTT calls these recipes) or create new ones.

These services are useful for enabling actions that Alexa can't do natively, but they're not perfect. For one thing, each service requires a unique action phrase that tells Alexa what to do. For example, IFTTT uses "Trigger, " and Yomi uses "Turn on." If you want Alexa to turn your home theater on using IFTTT and a linked-up Logitech Harmony Elite remote, you have to say "Alexa, Trigger turn on home theater."

Another limitation is that a cloud recipe can't trigger an action from your Alexa device. You can use Alexa to enable a recipe, but, you can't, for example, have Echo play Rock Around the Clock as part of an IFTTT wake-up recipe.

Because a command like the one above may need to access multiple cloud accounts at once, there's sometimes a delay of tens of seconds, and sometimes the commands just don't work. Also, if you've configured a lot of IFTTT recipes it's easy to forget the exact phrase that works, so user mistakes are common.

Amazon Echo Show

The newest addition to the Echo family, the Show adds a touchscreen and camera to the smart speaker, allowing you to make video calls, view security camera feeds, watch videos on YouTube and Amazon Prime Video, watch new video flash briefings, buy things from Amazon (of course), and more. The Echo Show is now available for pre-order for $229.99 and will ship at the end of June.

Amazon Echo Look

Another recent addition to the Echo family, the Echo Look is a camera with Alexa built-in that allows Alexa to act as your fashion consultant. You can have Alexa take photos and videos of your outfits to build out a personal lookbook, have it use machine learning to tell you which outfit looks better on you, and (unsurprisingly) have it recommend new clothes to buy. The Echo Look isn't widely available yet, but you can request an invitation to purchase one from Amazon for $199.99.

Amazon Echo Dot

Take the Echo, slice off the top, and you've got the Echo Dot. The Dot ditches the high-quality built-in speaker to cut down on cost, while still giving you all of Alexa's smarts. A smaller built-in speaker does let you talk to Alexa, but it's not good enough for streaming music. Instead, you can connect the Dot to speakers you already own via Bluetooth or an audio-out jack.

The Dot sells for $49, and Amazon offers a variety of bundles that package it with Bose speakers or other smart home products.

Amazon Tap

The Amazon Tap takes the Echo's core features and packs them into a portable Bluetooth speaker. Since it's battery-powered, the Tap isn't always listening like the Echo or Echo Dot. Instead, you have to press a mic button to speak to Alexa. However, a recent update does allow you to enable hands-free listening at the expense of an hour of battery life.

Even though it's portable, the Tap requires a WiFi connection to use Alexa (there's no LTE option), so if you're out and about, you'll need to use your smartphone as a mobile hotspot.

Amazon Fire TV

The Fire TV version of Alexa doesn't have all the same features as Alexa on the Echo, but it can still control smart home products and take advantage of Alexa Skills.

The main difference is the way you interact with Alexa. You need to have your TV on and speak to Alexa through the Fire TV Remote. There's no always-on listening mode, but that might be a positive if you have privacy concerns.

Amazon Fire TV Stick with Voice Remote

The Fire TV Stick with Voice Remote also offers Alexa, using the same remote interface. Alexa on Fire TV Stick offers the same features as Alexa on the Fire TV box and is the cheapest way to get the virtual assistant at just $50.

Amazon App

Want Alexa with you everywhere you go? Thanks to a recent update to the Amazon App for iPhone, the virtual assistant is now baked into Amazon's highly popular shopping app. It doesn't offer all the same features of Alexa on the Amazon Echo but does allow you to search the store for things to buy. Unfortunately, there's no word on when Alexa will come to the Android version of the app.

Huawei Mate 9

Huawei made headlines when it announced that its new Mate 9 smartphone would be the first phone with Alexa built-in. The phone runs Android and offers Google's suite of apps, but instead of offering Google Assistant, the company defected to Amazon for its virtual assistant. We haven't reviewed the phone yet, but it does offer two days of battery life and a Leica camera, all for around $580. Just be warned, it's only compatible with AT&T and T-Mobile.

Invoxia Triby

If you want to make your fridge smarter without shelling out thousands of dollars, then you should check out the Invoxia Triby. It's already out on the market and is now the first third-party device to offer Alexa integration.

The Triby has a built-in speaker for playing music, a screen that can display doodles made in the companion app, and the ability to make calls to phones running the app.

Ford Sync

Ford vehicles with the latest version of the Ford Sync infotainment system will get Alexa integration, putting the Echo's core features (plus some driving-related ones) right in the car. It's such a clever integration that it won one of our CES Editors' Choice Awards last year.

Insteon Hub

Insteon may not be as flashy as SmartThings and Wink, but the older ecosystem remains a compelling option (if frustratingly closed). Alexa can control products specifically through the Insteon Hub (2245-222).

Amazon's assistant won't work with any of Insteon's other hubs, including the Home Kit-compatible Insteon Hub Pro. With the 2245-222 and Alexa, you can control plugs, switches, lights, and wired thermostats.

Alarm.com Hub

Alarm.com is a dealer-installed smart home and security system — an unusual arrangement that takes a headache out of having to set up a smart home system yourself. At CES 2016, the company announced integration with the Amazon Echo, which will allow Alexa to control Alarm.com lighting products and thermostats. You can also use your voice to arm the security system.

Vivint Hub

Vivint is a professionally installed smart home and security solution that also announced Amazon Echo integration at CES 2016. With Vivint, Alexa can arm your security system and control lights, thermostats, garage doors, and even smart locks.

Philips Hue Go (via Hue Bridge)

The Philips Hue Go puts the color control of Hue bulbs into a rechargeable, portable light that puts out 300 lumens and lasts up to three hours on a charge. The only downside is that it requires a Philips Hue Bridge (included with the starter kits above) to connect it to the Hue app, and subsequently, Alexa.

Philips Friends of Hue Lighting Bloom (via Hue Bridge)

Part of the Friends of Hue lighting line, this color-changing bloom is another unusual fixture you can place in your home, but it lacks a built-in battery. You'll still need a Hue Bridge to take advantage of all this light has to offer, including the ability to control it with Alexa.

Cree Connected LED (via Smart Things Hub or Wink Hub)

The Cree Connected LED bulb is one of the most affordable and flexible bulbs on the market. They're priced competitively with Philips Hue White bulbs but work with just about any smart home hub. That makes them a better deal in the long run since it sets you up to start building a comprehensive smart home ecosystem.

Through a Smart Things or Wink hub, you'll be able to control these affordable bulbs with Alexa. Cree also offers a 5000K variant of the bulb.

Osram Lighting Smart Bulb (via Smart Things Hub or Wink Hub)

Osram Lighting bulbs don't change color, but they do offer adjustable color temperature for less than the LIFX White 800 bulbs. There many other products in the Lighting lineup, including a recessed, LED light, a color-changing light strip, and an outdoor lighting kit, but it's unclear if they all work with Alexa.

TCP Connected Smart Bulbs (via Smart Things Hub or Wink Hub)

TCP Connected bulbs are far from the best solution on the market. They require their additional hub and offer lackluster performance. But they do also work with Alexa if you connect them to a Smart Things or Wink Hub

Even though it's a professionally installed system, Vivint provides arguably the best voice control of any smart home system, though rivals are catching up quick.

Nexia Home Intelligence Bridge

Nexia is far from a name brand, but the smart home ecosystem works with a variety of Z-Wave smart home devices.

Like Alarm.com and Vivint, Nexia also recently announced Amazon Echo integration for its system but hasn't offered many details on which products will work with Alexa.

Universal Devices ISY Hubs

You've probably never heard of Universal Devices, but home automation geeks know the company for its Insteon-compatible ISY ("izzy") hubs.

The company offers two hubs: the ISY-994i Series and ISY-994iZw Series. Both offer Insteon compatibility, but the latter adds a Z-Wave radio for those devices.

Set up Alexa integration and you'll be able to control lights, door locks, thermostats, and device programs, which make changes to multiple devices at once.

Home Seer Home Controllers

Home Seer offers six different smart home controllers (or hubs) that are geared much more towards home automation geeks than average consumers.

With the Home Seer Amazon Echo integration, users can ask Alexa to control lights, locks, thermostats, garage doors, and security systems.

Simple Control Simple Hub

Simple Control is primarily focused on A/V and home theater control, but the company's powerful hub and app allow you to control many other devices including entire smart Things and Insteon systems.

The system isn't simple (or cheap), but it allows for a lot of customization. Due to Simple Control's A/V focus, Alexa can control TVs, and even change channels for you.

Almond Smart Home WiFi Routers

Instead of purchasing a separate smart home hub, Securifi's Almond routers double as smart home hubs and WiFi routers. Two of the Almond routers, Almond+ and Almond 2015, also work with Alexa and the Echo. With their integration, you'll be able to activate scenes and modes through Alexa that you've created with your Almond router.

Chapter 6

ALEXA FUNCTIONS AND LIMITATIONS.

Alexa functions

Alexa offers weather reports provided by AccuWeather and news provided by TuneIn from a variety of sources including local radio stations, NPR, and ESPN. Additionally, Alexa-supported devices stream music from the owner's Amazon Music accounts and have built-in support for Pandora and Spotify accounts. Alexa can play music from streaming services such as Apple Music and Google Play Music from a phone or tablet. Alexa can manage voice-controlled alarms, timers, and shopping and to-do lists, and can access Wikipedia articles. Alexa devices will respond to questions about items in the user's Google Calendar. As of November 2016, the Alexa Appstore had over 5,000 functions ("skills") available for users to download,[10] up from 1,000 functions in June 2016.

Home automation.

In the home automation space, Alexa can interact with devices from Belkin Wemo, ecobee, IFTTT, Insteon, LIFX, LightwaveRF,[13] Nest Thermostats, Philips Hue, Smart Things, Wink,[14][15] and Yonomi.The Home Automation feature was launched on April 8, 2015.

Ordering

Take-out food can be ordered using Alexa; as of May 2017 food ordering using Alexa is supported by Domino's Pizza, Grub hub, Pizza Hut, Seamless, and Wingstop.Also, users of Alexa in the UK can order meals via Just Eat. In early 2017, Starbucks announced a private beta for placing pick-up orders using Alexa. Also, users can order meals using Amazon Prime Now via Alexa in 20 major US cities.

Music

Alexa supports a multitude of subscription-based and free streaming services on Amazon devices. These streaming services include Prime Music, Amazon Music, Amazon Music Unlimited, TuneIn, iHeartRadio, Audible, Pandora, and Spotify Premium. However, some of these music services are not available on other Alexa-enabled products that are manufactured by companies' external of its services. This unavailability also includes Amazon's own Fire TV devices or tablets.

Alexa can stream media and music directly. To do this, Alexa's device should be linked to the Amazon account, which enables access to one's Amazon Music library, in addition to any audiobooks available in one's Audible library. Amazon Prime members have an additional ability to access stations, playlists, and over two million songs free of charge. Amazon Music Unlimited subscribers also have access to a list of millions of songs.

Amazon Music for PC allows one to play personal music from Google Play, iTunes, and others on an Alexa device. This can be done by uploading one's collection to My Music on Amazon from a computer. Up to 250 songs can be uploaded free of charge. Once this is done, Alexa can play this music and control playback through voice command options.

Sports

Alexa allows the user to hear updates on supported sports teams. A way to do this is by adding the sports team to the list created under Alexa's Sports Update app section.

The user can hear updates on up to 15 supported teams, of which consist of the following:

MLS - Major League Soccer EPL - English Premier League NBA - National Basketball Association NCAA men's basketball - National Collegiate Athletic Association UEFA Champions League - Union of European Football Association FA Cup - Football Association Challenge CupMLB - Major League Baseball NHL - National Hockey League NCAA FBS football.

National Collegiate Athletic Association: Football Bowl Subdivision NFL - National Football League German Bundesliga 2nd Division WNBA - Women's National Basketball Association German Bundesliga 1st Division

Messaging and Email.

Messages can be sent through multiple ways from Alexa's application. Alexa can deliver messages to a recipient's Alexa application, as well as to all of their Echo devices that are both supported and associated with their Amazon account. Alexa can send typed messages only from Alexa's app. If one sends a message from an associated Echo device, it will be sent as a voice message. Alexa cannot send attachments including videos and photos.

If there are multiple members of one's household, one's Alexa contacts are pooled across all of the devices that are registered to its associated account. However, within Alexa's app, one is only able to start conversations with its Alexa contacts. When accessed and supported by an Alexa app or Echo device, Alexa messaging is available to anyone in one's household. These messages can be heard by anyone with access in the household. This messaging feature does not yet contain a password protection or associated PIN. Anyone who has access to one's cell phone number can use this feature to contact them through their supported Alexa app or Echo device. The feature to block alerts for messages and calls is available temporarily by utilizing the Do Not Disturb feature.

Alexa Skills Kit.

Amazon allows developers to build and publish skills for Alexa using the Alexa Skills Kit. These skills are 3rd-party developed voice experiences that add to the capabilities of any Alexa-enabled device (such as the Echo). These skills are available for free download using the Alexa app. Skills are continuously being added to increase the capabilities available to the user. A "Smart Home Skill API" is available. All of the code runs in the cloud – nothing is on any user device. A developer can follow tutorials to learn how to build voice experiences for their new and existing applications quickly.

Alexa Voice Service

Amazon allows device manufacturers to integrate Alexa voice capabilities into their connected products by using the Alexa Voice Service (AVS), a cloud-based service that provides APIs for interfacing with Alexa. Products built using AVS have access to Alexa's growing list of capabilities including all of the Alexa Skills. AVS provides cloud-based automatic speech recognition (ASR) and natural language understanding (NLU). There are no fees for

companies looking to integrate Alexa into their products by using AVS.

The voice of Amazon Alexa is generated by a long short-term memory artificial neural network.

Advantages of Alexa

Alexa has many positive features. I have used the voice assistant on my phone, with the Amazon Echo speaker, and even with a radio, called the Triby, in my kitchen. One of the main benefits of Alexa is that the assistant understands almost everything I say. For chatbots, that's critical. Any bot worth using should understand natural language processing. If it doesn't, it will suffer a quick death on the market.

Alexa is also highly extensible. I use the assistant with a Vivint home security system and have a feature that lets me control the locks in my home. (As a security precaution, the feature only allows you to lock, not unlock your home.) That's a great integration, and chatbots need to follow this example. If a chatbot only works with a few basic services, like your calendar, it won't survive for long.

More than anything, Alexa saves time and improves your day. I use the Domino's feature at least once per month, as I can order a pizza by voice much faster than using any app. everything on Alexa seems to work smoothly, from getting the weather to getting a quick lowdown on the news. Chatbots need to follow suit.

Publish Your Metrics to Boost Advertising Revenue

Showcasing your traffic stats and true audience size can help you attract potential business partners, investors, and advertisers. After certifying your site, you can choose to publish your Certified Metrics including Unique Visitors and Page views on your site's public Site Overview page.

Monitor Your Site's Performance

If you've ever experienced a sharp downward trend in your site's traffic, you know it is crucial to isolate the cause quickly. Is the cause due to a problem on your site or an external event? Alexa Certified Metrics makes performance tracking easy by continually monitoring your site's uptime. We display your uptime next to your traffic graphs – allowing you to cross-correlate traffic trends with your site's availability and technical issues.

Count 100% of Your Real Traffic

By installing Alexa's Certify Code on your site, Alexa will begin directly measuring and reporting on your site's traffic. This provides you with invaluable insights into your site's performance. In contrast to other analytics services, such as Google Analytics, we ensure all of your site's traffic is being counted. We do this by reviewing your site every month and alerting you if pages of your site are missing the Certify Code. This is important because no code = no traffic data. As a result of our monthly site scans, you can feel confident that all of your site's traffic is included in your Certified Metrics.

Limitations

One of the biggest gripes Alexa owners have—even owners who are big fans of the system—is that it can receive only one command at a time. You can't say, "Alexa, turn on the living room and bedroom lights" unless you've already created a group called "Living room and bedroom." You can't say, "Alexa, play the Beatles and turn up the thermostat." Each command needs to be spoken separately. Even if you've created scenes, routines, or robots in your smart home hub app, you can directly address only individual devices or groups in Alexa.

Similarly, you can create a shopping list by telling Alexa to add firecrackers or beer to your list, but you must add each item separately. For example, instead of saying "Alexa, add firecrackers and beer to my shopping list," you have to say "Alexa, add firecrackers to my shopping list. Alexa, add beer to my shopping list." If you're creating a large shopping list, the process can get annoying, especially for other people in the room. Further, though Alexa nicely creates a shopping list in its app (that you can access when you're in the grocery store), you need to use an IFTTT recipe to create a version of the list for sharing or printing.

And although one of the favorite uses of Echo is to ask random questions, Alexa isn't Google. The system knows a lot, but what it can't answer outweighs what it can.

Owners of multiple Alexa devices, such as myself, have run into problems as a result of the limited number of wake words. Again, you can change the Echo's wake word, but you can use only "Alexa," "Amazon," "Echo," or "Computer." The far-field microphones on the Echo and Dot are so sensitive that if I address the Dot in my basement theater, and still have the basement door open, the Echo in the kitchen is likely to respond as well. Owners can change the wake word for each Alexa device, but it gets confusing to remember which one responds to "Alexa" and which one responds to "Echo." Amazon hopes to resolve this issue with the introduction of its new Echo Spatial Perception technology, which activates voice commands from one Echo device—the one closest to you—regardless of how many devices are in the room.

In addition to wake-word confusion, sometimes Alexa can't hear your request due to background noise or because it's playing music too loudly. Amazon has built-in noise-cancellation technology, but sometimes it falls short. The device also can't tell who is speaking or how many people are talking. If one person says "Alexa" while another person in the room says, "Pass me the hot sauce," your Echo may give you a bizarre response. (Though it's an occasional problem, Alexa has proven to be a better listener than my teenage children.) Amazon sends automatic firmware upgrades from time to time, and owners have reported performance changes after those updates. Sometimes those updates are improvements, and sometimes not, but you can't control when they arrive.

If you use your Echo or Dot primarily for music, and you're hoping for a whole-house music system similar to Sonos, you should stick with Sonos. Though Echos, Dots, and Taps will let you play music in every room, they can't synchronize their music the way a true whole-house music system can, because the stream to each speaker is independent—you can't group them and control a bunch of Echo together. You can't say, "Play the Misfits on all my speakers.

You have to go to each Alexa device and tell it to play music separately. Also, Amazon Prime's music rules let you play only one stream at the time, so if you're playing Prime Music in the living room, you'll need to use Pandora or Spotify for music in the kitchen. And if you use TuneIn for podcasts, Alexa may disappoint. Trying to find a particular podcast or episode via voice search can be frustrating. TuneIn stations may also become temporarily unavailable.

Alexa has a ways to go, however. One of the issues noticed lately is that the bot works with quite a few services but is far from even making a dent in the connected home market. I can raise and lower the temperature in my home by voice, but not with the Honeywell smart thermostats. (Update: Amazon recently added this feature as a skill in the Alexa app.)

Alexa works with the Sensi brand — but only after some configuration of both the hardware and the software. Chatbots that are truly useful will need to extend themselves far beyond a simple set of connections.

Another big gripe I have with Alexa is that it only works when I'm in my office. I have an Echo speaker there, and my phone with the Alexa app is usually tucked away somewhere (I use Skype at my desk with a headset). I should be able to talk to Alexa in any room, but it doesn't quite work that way yet. Compatibility is a big issue for any bot. Maybe they need to work on iOS and Android but also on BlackBerry devices and Windows phones. Bonus if a chatbot works on phones that are not even available anymore.

And, last but not least, Alexa can be temperamental. As we reported recently, the service was down for a while. I've personally experienced outrages at times. When reading a book, I've had the speaker fail a few times, which ruins the experience. A chatbot that crashes is a useless chatbot, especially as we're trying to adjust to the idea of using them. To make a good first impression, chatbots need to work almost perfectly.

www.ingramcontent.com/pod-product-compliance
Lightning Source LLC
LaVergne TN
LVHW022322060326
832902LV00020B/3612